CW00922293

How to access your on-line resources

Kaplan Financial students will have a MyKaplan account and these extra resources will be available to you online. You do not need to register again, as this process was completed when you enrolled. If you are having problems accessing online materials, please ask your course administrator.

If you are not studying with Kaplan and did not purchase your book via a Kaplan website, to unlock your extra online resources please go to www.en-gage.co.uk (even if you have set up an account and registered books previously). You will then need to enter the ISBN number (on the title page and back cover) and the unique pass key number contained in the scratch panel below to gain access.

You will also be required to enter additional information during this process to set up or confirm your account details.

If you purchased through the Kaplan Publishing website you will automatically receive an e-mail invitation to register your details and gain access to your content. If you do not receive the e-mail or book content, please contact Kaplan Publishing.

Your code and information

This code can only be used once for the registration of one book online. This registration and your online content will expire when the final sittings for the examinations covered by this book have taken place. Please allow one hour from the time you submit your book details for us to process your request.

Please scratch the film to access your unique code.

Please be aware that this code is case-sensitive and you will need to include the dashes within the passcode, but not when entering the ISBN.

CIMA

Case Study

Strategic Level

Study Text

KAPLAN PUBLISHING'S STATEMENT OF PRINCIPLES

LINGUISTIC DIVERSITY, EQUALITY AND INCLUSION

We are committed to diversity, equality and inclusion and strive to deliver content that all users can relate to.

We are here to make a difference to the success of every learner.

Clarity, accessibility and ease of use for our learners are key to our approach.

We will use contemporary examples that are rich, engaging and representative of a diverse workplace.

We will include a representative mix of race and gender at the various levels of seniority within the businesses in our examples to support all our learners in aspiring to achieve their potential within their chosen careers.

Roles played by characters in our examples will demonstrate richness and diversity by the use of different names, backgrounds, ethnicity and gender, with a mix of sexuality, relationships and beliefs where these are relevant to the syllabus.

It must always be obvious who is being referred to in each stage of any example so that we do not detract from clarity and ease of use for each of our learners.

We will actively seek feedback from our learners on our approach and keep our policy under continuous review. If you would like to provide any feedback on our linguistic approach, please use this form (you will need to enter the link below into your browser).

https://docs.google.com/forms/d/1YNo3A16mtXGTDIFJzgJhcu377QA4Q4ihUgfYvVKclF8/edit

We will seek to devise simple measures that can be used by independent assessors to randomly check our success in the implementation of our Linguistic Equality, Diversity and Inclusion Policy.

Published by: Kaplan Publishing UK

Unit 2 The Business Centre, Molly Millars Lane, Wokingham, Berkshire RG41 2QZ

Acknowledgements

We are grateful to the CIMA for permission to reproduce past examination questions and the official CIMA answers.

Notice

The text in this material and any others made available by any Kaplan Group company does not amount to advice on a particular matter and should not be taken as such. No reliance should be placed on the content as the basis for any investment or other decision or in connection with any advice given to third parties. Please consult your appropriate professional adviser as necessary.

Kaplan Publishing Limited and all other Kaplan group companies expressly disclaim all liability to any person in respect of any losses or other claims, whether direct, indirect, incidental, consequential or otherwise arising in relation to the use of such materials.

Kaplan is not responsible for the content of external websites. The inclusion of a link to a third party website in this text should not be taken as an endorsement.

Kaplan Publishing's learning materials are designed to help students succeed in their examinations. In certain circumstances, CIMA can make post-exam adjustment to a student's mark or grade to reflect adverse circumstances which may have disadvantaged a student's ability to take an exam or demonstrate their normal level of attainment (see CIMA's Special Consideration policy). However, it should be noted that students will not be eligible for special consideration by CIMA if preparation for or performance in a CIMA exam is affected by any failure by their tuition provider to prepare them properly for the exam for any reason including, but not limited to, staff shortages, building work or a lack of facilities etc.

Similarly, CIMA will not accept applications for special consideration on any of the following grounds:

- failure by a tuition provider to cover the whole syllabus

- failure by the student to cover the whole syllabus, for instance as a result of joining a course part way through

- failure by the student to prepare adequately for the exam, or to use the correct pre-seen material

- errors in the Kaplan Official Study Text, including sample (practice) questions or any other Kaplan content or

- errors in any other study materials (from any other tuition provider or publisher).

British Library Cataloguing in Publication Data

A catalogue record for this book is available from the British Library.

ISBN: 978-1-83996-243-1

Printed and bound in Great Britain

Contents

Introduction

Acknowledgements

Every effort has been made to contact the holders of copyright material, but if any here have been inadvertently overlooked the publishers will be pleased to make the necessary arrangements at the first opportunity.

How to use the Materials

 Test your understanding – Following key points and definitions are exercises which give the opportunity to assess the understanding of these core areas. Within the work book the answers to these sections are left blank, explanations to the questions can be found within the online version which can be hidden or shown on screen to enable repetition of activities.

 Illustration – to help develop an understanding of topics and the test your understanding exercises the illustrative examples can be used.

Quality and accuracy are of the utmost importance to us so if you spot an error in any of our products, please send an email to mykaplanreporting@kaplan.com with full details.

Our Quality Coordinator will work with our technical team to verify the error and take action to ensure it is corrected in future editions.

Exam Introduction

To complete the CIMA qualification and be able to use the designatory letters of ACMA and CGMA, candidates for this prestigious award need to achieve three things:

- attain the entry requirements for the professional level qualification

- study for and complete the relevant professional level assessments and examinations

- complete three years of relevant practical experience

This text concentrates on the second of these requirements, and in particular to study for and complete the Strategic level case study exam.

Overview of exam

The case study exam will be available four times a year. The purpose of this exam is to consolidate learning at each level by reflecting real life work situations. The exam is human marked.

This approach allows a wide range of knowledge and skills to be tested including research and analysis, presentation of information and communication skills whilst still ensuring competence in key skills.

CIMA believe that this format will provide the commitment to delivering the competencies which employers desire thereby improving 'employability'.

For example, the Strategic level case study exam will be set within a simulated business context, placing the candidate in the job role matched to the competency level. In the case of the Strategic level, the job role is that of a senior finance manager, reporting to the highest levels of management within the organisation. The focus will be on the long-term, involving the strategic direction of the organisation.

The exam is intended to replicate "a day in the life" of a finance professional operating at the strategic level and provide a simulated environment for candidates to demonstrate the required level of proficiency in each of the competency areas. Consequently, the exam will be set and marked according to the weightings for each core activity at the level.

The case study exam is 3 hours in duration and is made up of a series of timed tests or tasks. This makes the case study exam different from most exams you will have sat to date – once you have submitted a particular task (or the time limit is reached, whichever is sooner) you will be moved on and will not be able to return to that task. This should reduce the problem of not completing the paper but does mean you will need to be very disciplined when attempting each task.

Candidates will be provided with access to pre-seen information approximately seven weeks before the real exam.

Assessment aims and strategy

The Case Study Examination tests the knowledge, skills and techniques from the three pillars within one simulated scenario and is taken at the end of each level of the CIMA Professional Qualification. Candidates are given a fictional Case Study before the examination and are expected to give solutions to the situations and challenges presented within the examination – based on the knowledge and skills acquired from the three subjects. The Case Study mimics their role in a real-work scenario, at each level of the qualification.

The case study is three hours long. The case study will include both pre-seen and unseen material, the latter being made available during the examination. They will incorporate short written answers, emails, letters and any form of appropriate communication required within the tasks set.

The focus is on application, analysis and evaluation which are levels 3, 4 and 5 of the CIMA hierarchy of verbs (see below).

Simulated business issues in the case studies provide candidates with the opportunity to demonstrate their familiarity with the context and interrelationships of the level's technical content. This reflects the cross functional abilities required in the workplace. Skills will include research, analysis, presentation of both financial and nonfinancial information and communication skills.

Feedback will be provided to candidates with their results. Exam sittings for the case studies will occur every three months. Candidates must have completed or be exempt from the three objective tests at a particular level before attempting the relevant integrated case study.

Core activities and assessment outcomes

Within each Strategic Case Study Examination, five "core activities" will be assessed. These core activities represent the tasks that are most frequent, critical and important to the senior finance professional role.

The five core activities are:

A   Develop business strategy.

B   Evaluate the business ecosystem and business environment.

C   Recommend financing strategies.

D   Evaluate and mitigate risk.

E   Recommend and maintain a sound control environment.

The core activities are linked to associated assessment outcomes expressed in terms of 'I Can' statements that speak directly to the skills and competencies that drive the employability of successful learners.

The core activities require and draw together the knowledge, skills and techniques acquired while studying for Objective Tests and combining them with the mindset of a CIMA finance professional.

Each core activity is translated into a number of "assessment outcomes". These are a clear assertion of what a CIMA qualified finance professional should be able to do when the Examination has been completed and what the assessment will be designed to measure. Case Study assessment outcomes will be synoptic

These are discussed in more detail in chapters 1 and 2.

Assessing skills – the CIMA verb hierarchy

CIMA has adopted a skill framework for the assessments based on the revised Bloom's Taxonomy of Education Objectives. Bloom's Taxonomy classifies a continuum of skills that learners are expected to know and demonstrate.

The case study exam will focus on Levels 3, 4 and 5.

Skill level	Verbs used	Definition
Level 5 Evaluation How you are expected to use your learning to evaluate, make decisions or recommendations	Advise	Counsel, inform or notify
	Assess	Evaluate or estimate the nature, ability or quality of
	Evaluate	Appraise or assess the value of
	Recommend	Propose a course of action
	Review	Assess and evaluate in order, to change if necessary
Level 4 Analysis How you are expected to analyse the detail of what you have learned	Align	Arrange in an orderly way
	Analyse	Examine in detail the structure of
	Communicate	Share or exchange information
	Compare and contrast	Show the similarities and/or differences between
	Develop	Grow and expand a concept
	Discuss	Examine in detail by argument
	Examine	Inspect thoroughly
	Interpret	Translate into intelligible or familiar terms
	Monitor	Observe and check the progress of
	Prioritise	Place in order of priority or sequence for action
	Produce	Create or bring into existence
Level 3 Application How you are expected to apply your knowledge	Apply	Put to practical use
	Calculate	Ascertain or reckon mathematically
	Conduct	Organise and carry out
	Demonstrate	Prove with certainty or exhibit by practical means
	Prepare	Make or get ready for use
	Reconcile	Make or prove consistent/compatible
Level 2 Comprehension What you are expected to understand	Describe	Communicate the key features of
	Distinguish	Highlight the differences between
	Explain	Make clear or intelligible/state the meaning or purpose of
	Identify	Recognise, establish or select after consideration
	Illustrate	Use an example to describe or explain something
Level 1 Knowledge What you are expected to know	List	Make a list of
	State	Express, fully or clearly, the details/facts of
	Define	Give the exact meaning of
	Outline	Give a summary of

How to use the material

These Official CIMA learning materials brought to you by CIMA and Kaplan Publishing have been carefully designed to make your learning experience as easy as possible and give you the best chances of success in your Case Study Examinations.

This Study Text has been designed with the needs of home study and distance learning candidates in mind. However, the Study Text is also ideal for fully taught courses.

The aim of this textbook is to walk you through the stages to prepare for, and to answer, the requirements of the Case Study Examination.

Practical hints and realistic tips are given throughout the book making it easy for you to apply what you've learned in this text to your actual Case Study Exam.

Where sample solutions are provided, they must be viewed as just one interpretation of the case. One key aspect, which you must appreciate early in your studies, is that there is no single 'correct' solution.

Your own answer might reach different conclusions, and give greater emphasis to some issues and less emphasis to others, but score equally as well if it demonstrates the required skills.

If you work conscientiously through the official CIMA Study Text according to the guidelines above, as well as analysing the pre-seen information in full, you will be giving yourself an excellent chance of success in your examination. Good luck with your studies!

Planning

To begin with, formal planning is essential to get the best return from the time you spend studying. Estimate how much time in total you are going to need for each subject you are studying for the Case Study Examination.

With your study material before you, decide which chapters you are going to study in each week, which weeks you will devote to practising past exams, and which weeks you will spend becoming familiar with your case study pre-seen material.

Prepare a written schedule summarising the above and stick to it! Students are advised to refer to articles published regularly in CIMA's magazine (Financial Management), the student e-newsletter (Velocity) and on the CIMA website, to ensure they are up to date with relevant issues and topics.

Tips for effective studying

1   Aim to find a quiet and undisturbed location for your study, and plan as far as possible to use the same period of time each day. Getting into a routine helps to avoid wasting time. Make sure that you have all the materials you need before you begin so as to minimise interruptions.

2   Store all your materials in one place, so that you do not waste time searching for items every time you want to begin studying. If you have to pack everything away after each study period, keep your study materials in a box, or even a suitcase, which will not be disturbed until the next time.

3   Limit distractions. To make the most effective use of your study periods you should be able to apply total concentration, so turn off all entertainment equipment, set your phones to message mode, and put up your 'do not disturb' sign.

4   Your timetable will tell you which topic to study. However, before diving in and becoming engrossed in the finer points, make sure you have an overall picture of all the areas that need to be covered by the end of that session. After an hour, allow yourself a short break and move away from your Study Text. With experience, you will learn to assess the pace you need to work at. Each study session should focus on component learning outcomes – the basis for all questions.

5   Work carefully through a chapter, making notes as you go. When you have covered a suitable amount of material, vary the pattern by attempting a practice question. When you have finished your attempt, make notes of any mistakes you made, or any areas that you failed to cover or covered more briefly. Be aware that all component learning outcomes will be tested in each examination.

6   Make notes as you study, and discover the techniques that work best for you. Your notes may be in the form of lists, bullet points, diagrams, summaries, 'mind maps', or the written word, but remember that you will need to refer back to them at a later date, so they must be intelligible. If you are on a taught course, make sure you highlight any issues you would like to follow up with your lecturer.

7   Organise your notes. Make sure that all your notes, calculations etc. can be effectively filed and easily retrieved later.

Relevant practical experience

In order to become a Chartered Global Management Accountant (ACMA, CGMA), you need a minimum of three years' verified relevant work-based practical experience.

Read the 'Applying for Membership' brochure for full details of the practical experience requirements (PER).

Information concerning formulae and tables will be provided via the CIMA website, www.cimaglobal.com.

Introduction to case study exams

Chapter learning objectives

- To gain an overview of the case study exam, its purpose, structure and the process involved.

1 The structure of the CIMA Strategic Level

Each level of CIMA's professional qualification consists of three objective test 'pillar' exams, followed by the Case Study Examination.

You can only attempt the Case Study Examination after all objective tests for the level have been completed or if exemptions have been given.

For the 2019 syllabus the three Strategic level pillar exams are as follows:

- E3 – Strategic Management
- P3 – Risk Management
- F3 – Financial Strategy

The objective tests for each of these individual subjects ensure the acquisition of the breadth of knowledge, skills and techniques that provide the foundation for approaching the Case Study Examination.

2 Why a Case Study Examination?

The CIMA Case Study Examinations are 'capstone' examinations designed to demonstrate mastery of previously acquired knowledge, skills and techniques and the drawing together of these to provide solutions to unstructured, synoptic problems.

Each synoptic assessment combines the content covered in all three pillar subjects at the level into a single assessment. Its aim is the "undoing" of the pillar and subject divisions of the syllabus and the application of knowledge, skills and techniques to the type of problems that you might encounter in the workplace in a role matched to the appropriate level of the qualification.

The examination uses a Case Study to provide a rich, immersive scenario to prepare and to provide a context for the tasks in the examination. The scenarios are developed around today's modern business environment and the challenges that you will face – allowing you to demonstrate the 'core activities' that have been identified by employers as critical.

Examination tasks will be practical and applied, not theoretical or academic. To be successful, you will have to perform these core activities in the same way and to the same standards that would be valid and valued in the workplace.

The Case Study Examination is thus an attempt to simulate workplace problem solving, and allows examiners to move one step closer to the assessment of competence than is possible with objective test questions. It is a test of both professional competence and, by implication, employability.

In addition, the purpose of the Case Study Examination is to assess your proficiency in those specific skills that are less likely to be automated.

The purpose of this text is to suggest how you might prepare for the examination by developing and practising your skills. Since the examination tests a range of different skills, preparing for this examination needs to be different from studying for a 'traditional' examination.

3 Your role

Each case study exam will be set within a simulated business context, placing the candidate in the job role matched to the competency level.

In the case of the strategic level your role is that of a senior finance manager reporting to the highest levels of management, either an individual director or the board of directors as a whole.

This role can be broken down as follows:

- A senior finance manager advising the organisation's leaders in the development of business strategy to create value is required to evaluate strategic options, paying due attention to the organisation's ecosystem. Risk management is a significant part of the overall responsibility, including cyber risks.

- There is a duty to advise on issues relating to corporate governance. They are important both because of the reputational risks arising from poor governance and the threats to the well-being of internal and external stakeholders when boards are poorly structured and badly managed. As an important element of this, the senior finance manager is frequently involved in the evaluation of the control environment and the management of internal audit. The need to manage control is crucial given the increasing dangers arising from cyber risks.

- The frequent requirement to support strategic decision-making may require the formulation of models and other methods of justifying and legitimating decisions. The senior finance manager is also involved in the raising of finance from suitable sources in order to ensure that new strategic projects are adequately resourced.

- The business case for digitisation and the manner in which the entity creates partnerships for ensuring strategic success must be understood, as must the operation of capital markets in determining value.

- The senior finance manager advises on matters that involve considerable judgement and that may have a significant effect on stakeholders and therefore must adhere to high standards of professionalism and ethics in the course of their duties.

In summary, the Strategic level focuses on the long term and the identification, evaluating and implementation of successful strategies. The Strategic Case Study examination expects the learner to think and respond like a senior finance manager.

4 The exam 'blueprints'

For the first time, CIMA has released blueprints for its Professional Qualification Examination. The intent is that blueprints will demystify the examination — giving greater clarity on examinable topics; assessment approach, design and weightings; and learner expectations.

The Case Study Examination blueprint contains the following:

- **Core activities** – Business-related tasks that are common to the role being simulated and valued by employers which, if performed satisfactorily, enables the demonstration of the assessment outcomes.

- **Assessment outcomes** – A clear assertion of what a CIMA qualified finance professional can do when the Examination has been completed and what the assessment will be designed to measure. Case Study assessment outcomes will be synoptic.

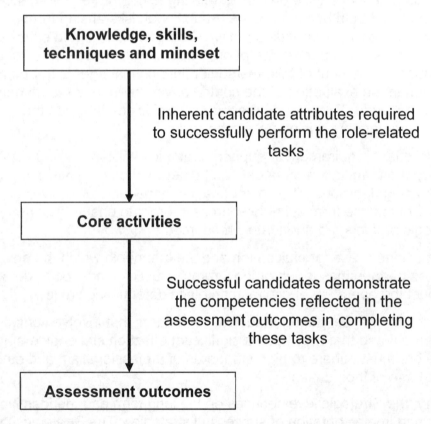

All core activities will be assessed in each form of the examination in line with the weightings. A sample of related assessment outcomes will be tested.

Blueprints are discussed in more detail in chapter 2.

5 The exam process

5.1 Overview

The examination is three hours long. A 15-minute tutorial is available before the start of the examination to allow candidates to familiarise themselves with the test driver.

The examination has three sections (tasks), which are each 1 hour long. All sections are equally weighted. Candidates may finish a section early and move on to the next but cannot return to previous sections in the time remaining.

There may be more than one sub-task within each section and an indication of how long to spend on each sub-task will be given to allow candidates to manage their time. If no weighting is given, then candidates should assume that the sub-tasks are equally weighted.

For example, the first exam variant of the sample prototype paper shows the following instructions:

Section (task)	Time for section (minutes)	Number of answer screens	Number of sub-tasks	% time to spend on each sub-task
1	60	1	2	(a) 55% (b) 45%
2	60	1	2	(a) 55% (b) 45%
3	60	1	3	(a) 60% (b) 20% (c) 20%

More than one core activity will normally (but not always) be assessed in each section/task and the order of core activities and assessment outcomes in the blueprint does not reflect how these might be structured in the examination.

For each sitting there are a number of variants, so different students will not necessarily face the same exam tasks. You are not permitted to discuss any aspects of the variant you sat until after the exam window has finished. The marking and moderation processes ensure that no advantage is gained from sitting one particular variant rather than another.

5.2 The pre-seen

The exam is based on:

- pre-seen material issued in advance of the exam day, supplemented by
- additional, previously unseen material given to you in the exam room.

From the May 2020 sitting onwards, one pre-seen will be used over two exam windows, giving candidates the opportunity to re-sit using the same pre-seen. The pre-seen will be shared as follows:

- May / August
- November / February

CIMA releases the pre-seen material approximately seven weeks before the first examination. This is posted on the student area of the CIMA website (www.cimaglobal.com) and it is your responsibility to download it and to print off a copy.

The pre-seen material is an introductory scenario to set the scene for the case study, together with accounting and financial information. The pre-seen material is an extended scenario consisting of approximately ten exhibits giving information about a business organisation.

You will be taking on the role of a management accountant who works for the organisation, and your responses to the tasks will usually be addressed to your superior.

5.3 The unseen

In the examination you will be provided with the following.

- An on-screen version of the pre-seen material
- Additional new unseen material, which contains both triggers (new information) and tasks (what you need to do)
- Space to complete your answers
- An on-screen calculator (although candidates are permitted to take their own calculators as long as it's a CIMA approved model.)
- Reference materials (Present value tables, Cumulative present value tables and Normal distribution tables)
- A notepad and pen for planning and workings along with an on-screen scratch pad.

The unseen material will be a continuation of the pre-seen and will usually bring the scenario up to date. In many cases there is a 'twist' in the unseen i.e. a development that students might not have anticipated from the pre-seen. The unseen may focus on a number of issues that appeared in the pre-seen or it may just focus on one or two; either way it will provide the basis for the content of your answers.

A common mistake made by weaker students is that they place too much emphasis on their analysis of the pre-seen material and do not develop the information in the unseen material adequately. The key points to be referred to in your answer should be driven by the new information in the unseen material.

5.4 Triggers and tasks

Each section in the unseen material will begin with a **trigger.**

This will be information provided as an introduction to the work that you are required to complete.

The information may be in the form of a briefing by your superior, a newspaper article, some financial information or extracts from internal reports. You will be expected to integrate this new information with the analysis you have performed on the pre-seen material to produce a coherent and well informed response.

Within each section of the examination, there will then be a **task** or tasks that you will be asked to perform, usually by your superior. These tasks will require different types of response, although usually reports, briefing notes and emails.

Word processing capabilities will be provided within the test driver to allow the formatting and presentation of responses in a professional manner. From 2019, this includes the ability to use tables to put together a response. For full details of the word processing functionality and to try this in advance of the examination, a tutorial is available on cimaglobal.com.

There is a time limit attached to each task and you will have a clock showing the time remaining in the corner of your screen. Once you have submitted a task (or the time limit is reached, whichever is sooner) you will not be able to return to that task. This should reduce the problem of not completing the paper but does mean you will need to be disciplined when attempting each task.

If you feel that you do not need all of the time on an earlier task, then moving forwards prematurely will not allow you extra time on later tasks – the extra time will be lost. Given this, it is always advisable to use the full time allocated to each task to recheck that you have answered the question requirement in full and that you have related your response to the specific context of the case.

A walkthrough of the prototype sample exam will be carried out in chapters 3 to 5.

5.5 Calculations

Examination tasks will not be set that require specific calculations.

However, candidates should, wherever possible, show how they have used and interpreted data from the pre-seen and the new information presented during the examination and/or undertook analysis or calculations to support their responses. Analysis should almost certainly be wholly or largely narrative or explanation. Candidates can sometimes supplement that narrative by offering simple calculations and explaining the results.

6   Marking

6.1   'Three level' marking

The Case Study Examinations are human marked using a holistic 'three level' approach for each task, enabling markers to give credit for all relevant points, even if not mentioned in the indicative answer.

For example, in the February 2020 exam, task 1 (a) of variant 1, worth 8 marks, asked students to do the following:

"Evaluate the argument that the reputational risk associated with our environmental impact should have been identified and managed before Planetguard created its online petition."

The published indicative answer was accompanied by the following marking grid:

Trait			
Evaluation of threat to reputational risk	**Level**	**Descriptor**	**Marks**
		No rewardable material	0
	Level 1	Identifies a limited range of realistic threats to reputation.	1-2
	Level 2	Offers some evaluation of the Board's ability to identify realistic threats to reputation.	3-5
	Level 3	Evaluates the Board's ability to identify realistic threats to reputation.	6-8

Markers will first assess which level to place your answers in, and then decide how many marks it is worth within the level concerned.

The lessons to be learned

The key differences between the levels are

*   Number of points made.

*   Understanding the examiner's use of the verb **evaluate**.

*   The extent to which you answered the question set – in this case, **evaluate** the Board's ability to **identify** and **manage** threats to the company's reputation.

Make sure your answers address these issues.

6.2 The 'marginally competent' student

During 2016 CIMA disclosed further information on how the pass mark is set and the importance of identifying the 'marginally competent' candidate.

The process

A detailed process was revealed that involves the following:

(1) A panel of experts debates the tasks within a variant to decide what should be expected from a student deemed competent for this task. This debate does not focus on a perfect answer but, instead, asks what would be expected of a CIMA student (or member) in practice – what is the minimum expected if we were considering employing them, for example.

(2) A sample of student scripts is then discussed and the scripts ranked. This is repeated and refined until the "marginally competent student" is identified. This student deserves to pass (but only just!) as they would be employable and have the skills expected of a CIMA student or member in the real world.

(3) The marks earned by this script are then used to set the pass mark and standardise the overall marking system. This ensures that students are not disadvantaged if they sit a "harder" variant.

In short, candidates should be reassured that CIMA goes to great lengths to ensure that there is no advantage or disadvantage to sitting one variant rather than another.

The lessons to be learned

When answering a task in the exam, you should take the same approach as if the exam was part of a job interview and ask yourself what would be required to get the job.

Your employer would be less impressed by you showing off knowledge but much more impressed that you can answer a question asked, apply your comments to the company's specific circumstances and make practical, relevant suggestions. Make sure your answers do this!

Demonstrating soft skills

In an article written for CIMA's website, the examiners made the following comments on the need for candidates to demonstrate so-called 'soft skills':

In a role simulation exam, it is critical that the candidate inhabits the role and the scenario in order to perform as well as possible. Applying technical knowledge and skills gained to the scenario together with the professional or "soft" skills that are critical for success in the workplace will enable candidates to demonstrate that they have achieved the core activities set out in the blueprint and can apply these in the context of the business, providing the best responses to the tasks.

These professional or soft skills are useful in any professional setting and include skills such as:

- *Communication*

- *Awareness of the digital ecosystem*

- *Professional scepticism*

- *Provide leadership*

- *Professional judgement*

- *Ethics and professionalism*

- *Business awareness.*

These skills are not tested directly (and marks are not specifically allocated to them), but they should be drawn upon when developing an answer plan. Applying these skills will support you in responding to a task and aid you in producing an answer that is relevant, provides the best solution for the simulated organisation and the issues it is facing and, consequently, achieves the highest marks available (that is, meeting the level 3 descriptors in the marking guides).

Questions need not necessarily – and likely will not – refer to a specific mindset skill in order to make it relevant. For example, a question might summarise a subordinate's explanation for a disappointing performance. A good candidate might apply professional scepticism in evaluating the validity of the explanation. If the question asks for a recommended response then the candidate might consider the leadership issues associated with alternatives. In some circumstances a reprimand might be in order and in others it might be preferable to offer support and encouragement.

Mindset and soft skills can be developed through practice. Reflecting on personal experiences at work, reading the business news and even attempting past case study exams are all ways to develop an understanding of what might work in any given set of circumstances.

6.3 A scaled score

Incorporating the 'marginally competent' student exercise and to ensure equity between exam variants, your mark will be adjusted to give a 'scaled score' out of 150 with 80 and above being a pass.

6.4 Feedback and 'grade descriptors'

Feedback on performance against each core activity will be provided so that learners know their areas of weakness for further study. (Note: there is no requirement to obtain a pass or meet a minimum threshold for each core activity – it is the overall mark that matters.)

In addition to the wording of core activities and assessment objectives, CIMA has published 'grade descriptors' to give you more insight into the skills required to pass. It is these that are used to feedback performance to students.

For example, the grade descriptors for core activity A are as follows:

Core activity	Assessment outcome	If you met the exam level passing standard for each of the core activities, you can generally be described using some or all of the following characteristics:
A. Develop business strategy	1. I can use evaluate strategic options (digital and otherwise). 2. I can recommend strategic decisions (digital and otherwise). 3. I can evaluate potential acquisitions and divestment opportunities. 4. I can recommend responses to opportunities and threats arising from digital technologies.	• Communicates strategic decisions and evaluation of strategic options clearly. • Demonstrates understanding of the business model and its environment, including digital ecosystems and disruptive businesses, in the development of business strategy. • Applies professional scepticism when recommending responses to opportunities and threats arising from digital technologies. • Demonstrates leadership when evaluating and advising on strategic decisions. • Demonstrates professional judgement and business awareness in the development of business strategy. • Demonstrates ethics and professionalism in the evaluation of strategic options and in the recommendation of strategic decisions. • Demonstrates technical understanding of the tools and techniques used to evaluate strategy.

Note that the verbs used in the third column (grade descriptors) are different from those in the second (assessment outcomes). This is designed to show how the 'softer skills' enable and support the achievements of the assessment outcomes and core activities within the simulation. It's intended to draw out the importance of these skills to support producing the best, most applied and plausible answers within the simulation.

The two columns are complementary and should be read in conjunction.

If in the exam, you score enough marks for the tasks relating to core activity A, then your feedback will show that you are 'proficient'.

On the other hand, if you fail to develop your answers sufficiently, then the feedback will show the following:

Core activity	Rating	*You were below the passing standard for this core activity. This is because you did not demonstrate some or all of the following characteristics:*
A. Develop business strategy	Not proficient	• Communicates strategic decisions and evaluation of strategic options clearly. • Demonstrates understanding of the business model and its environment, including digital ecosystems and disruptive businesses, in the development of business strategy. • Applies professional scepticism when recommending responses to opportunities and threats arising from digital technologies. • Demonstrates leadership when evaluating and advising on strategic decisions. • Demonstrates professional judgement and business awareness in the development of business strategy. • Demonstrates ethics and professionalism in the evaluation of strategic options and in the recommendation of strategic decisions. • Demonstrates technical understanding of the tools and techniques used to evaluate strategy.

The lessons to be learned

Make sure your answer demonstrates the 'soft skills' shown in the final column:

- Have you communicated clearly?

- Have you related your comments to the specific circumstances of the company in the scenario, thus demonstrating 'business awareness' and an 'understanding of the business model'?

- Have you evaluated the extent to which the technique being discussed, such as participation, is useful for the company in the scenario, thus demonstrating 'professional scepticism'?

7   Summary

You should now have a basic understanding of how the case study works. All of the ideas presented in this chapter will be developed further in the remainder of this textbook.

Next steps:

(1)   It is a good idea to register with Pearson Vue to see the online version of the Question Tutorial exam as this will allow you become more familiar with the look and feel of the exam. All the relevant material from the Question Tutorial exam has been reproduced in this textbook but it is important to recognise that the CIMA case study examinations are dynamic and shouldn't be viewed as equivalent to a static paper exam.

(2)   Think about the date on which you will sit the exam and work backwards to create a sensible and achievable study timetable.

(3)   You need to ensure that your technical knowledge is up to date / full especially if the OTQ exams were sat a while ago.

It might be worth locating and gathering together any materials you already have from the supporting technical subjects (E3, P3 and F3). We will show you in later chapters how you may need to use these materials.

Core activities and assessment outcomes

Chapter learning objectives

- To understand the core activities and assessment outcomes required for the case study exam.

1   Core Activities

In some respects, one could argue that everything covered in E3, F3 and P3 was still relevant for the Case Study Examination. However, to make such a daunting proposition clearer and more accessible, the blueprint defines the following core activities:

	Core Activity	Weighting
A	Develop business strategy.	15 – 25%
B	Evaluate the business ecosystem and business environment.	15 – 25%
C	Recommend financing strategies.	15 – 25%
D	Evaluate and mitigate risk.	15 – 25%
E	Recommend and maintain a sound control environment.	15 – 25%

As stated in chapter 1, **all** core activities will be assessed in each form of the examination in line with the weightings.

These core activities are linked to associated assessment outcomes expressed in terms of 'I Can' statements that speak directly to the skills and competencies that drive the employability of successful learners.

At first sight it may seem that core activities A and B are driven mainly by E3 knowledge and activities, C by F3 and D and E by P3. However, for a proper understanding of how the different technical papers might be assessed in the core activities, attention must be paid to the accompanying assessment outcomes.

2 Assessment outcomes

Assessment outcomes translate core activities into a range of "I can" statements that, in case study, effectively give you the basis of the wordings for exam tasks.

Given this, it is vital that you look at the assessment outcomes and make sure you feel confident that you could answer a task worded in this way. The full list is as follows:

	Core Activities	Assessment outcomes
A	Develop business strategy.	I can evaluate strategic options (digital and otherwise).
		I can recommend strategic decisions (digital and otherwise).
		I can evaluate potential acquisitions and divestment opportunities.
		I can recommend responses to opportunities and threats arising from digital technologies.
B	Evaluate business ecosystem and business environment.	I can select and apply suitable strategic analytical tools.
		I can conduct an analysis of stakeholder needs and recommend appropriate responses.
		I can recommend appropriate responses to changes in the business ecosystem.
		I can recommend KPIs that encourage sound strategic management.
		I can recommend responses to economic, political and currency risks.
C	Recommend financing strategies.	I can recommend suitable sources of finance.
		I can recommend dividend policy.
		I can recommend and apply business valuation models.
D	Evaluate and mitigate risk.	I can evaluate risks and recommend responses and can maintain the corporate risk register.
		I can identify ethical dilemmas and recommend suitable responses. I can evaluate and mitigate cyber risks.
		I can recommend internal controls.

E	Recommend and maintain a sound control environment.	I can apply internal audit resources.
		I can recommend appropriate controls and evaluate the implications of compliance failures.
		I can recommend responses to the threats arising from poor governance.

In the next section we will look at how these have been examined in the real exam. Given the syllabus changes in 2019, some tasks in past exams are no longer relevant, so we have focussed on ones that are still indicative of what you might face in your exam.

3   Examples of tasks from the May 2019 exam.

3.1 Summary of pre-seen scenario

To fully appreciate examples from recent real exams it is necessary to have a basic understanding of the case.

The pre-seen for the May 2019 Strategic Case Study involves a company called Denby Healthcare. It is the second-largest private hospital group in Keeland, and reports in K$.

Industry background

Keeland is an economically developed country with high employment levels. The provision of healthcare is state-funded, with hospitals and GP surgeries paid for out of taxes. Despite a large proportion of overall state revenues being spent on healthcare, demand still outstrips supply, and hospitals struggle to meet demand. This is because of 3 principal factors:

1   Advances in preventive medicine resulting from research. This means that more time and investment is needed for diagnosis, consultations, testing, and discussing results;

2   Increased life expectancy and an ageing population;

3   Lack of alternative providers in respect of critical care services for the extremely ill.

Waiting times are a key expectation, and the Keeland government has made it mandatory that all referrals for public hospital treatment will be completed within 15 weeks.

In addition to public hospitals, there are also a number of private hospitals in Keeland. People are prepared to go private for a number of reasons: convenience (shorter waiting times and more flexibility over timing of appointments); availability of treatments (private hospitals may have more advanced equipment, or offer services that the state will not pay for, such as certain cosmetic surgeries); comfort (rooms and food are often of higher quality in private hospitals); and, for foreign patients, because Keeland offers better healthcare than is available at home.

Private hospitals do not offer all the services that public hospitals do. For example, there are no Accident & Emergency (A&E) services in the private sector, nor is there intensive care. A&E is too expensive to operate, and there is no demand for intensive care in the private sector as the public hospitals would see to such patients immediately.

There are 3 private hospital groups in Keeland, all of which offer similar standards of care and healthcare services: Bronty Health is the largest with 48 hospitals; then Denby, with 43 hospitals; and thirdly Postar Primary Care, with 32. These are the only full-scale private hospitals, and each has a presence throughout Keeland.

They each derive revenue from 4 key sources:

1   From insurance companies, who refer patients under private health schemes

2   Self-pay (Keeland) i.e. from Keeland residents who choose to pay for private healthcare

3   Foreign patients i.e. from non-Keeland residents who choose Keeland for better healthcare than they can get at home

4   KHS patients. This is where the Keeland Health Service (KHS) refers patients to private hospitals in order to meet the maximum waiting period of 15 weeks imposed by the government. The KHS pays the private hospital charges for such patients.

Professional staff consists of senior doctors, junior doctors and nurses. Senior doctors work for both the KHS and also private hospitals, with part time contracts of employment with each. Junior doctors and nurses are full-time employees of their chosen hospitals.

Denby Healthcare

Denby was founded in the early 1980s by several senior doctors, all of whom have subsequently retired. The company achieved listed status in the 1990s. Denby has grown to have 43 hospitals and 23,500 staff; this has been by both organic means and also taking over smaller hospitals.

Denby's strategy is based on achieving and maintaining a reputation for clinical excellence. Staffing is the most important element of patient care, and so the company looks to attract and motivate the best employees.

It also seeks to maximise revenues earned from KHS hospital referrals. This can only be achieved if the quality of healthcare provided by Denby meets expectation, and also if Denby is able to meet the cost and flexibility expectations of KHS hospitals.

Profit margins in private hospitals can be considerable. An example is given of a hip replacement operation, on which the mark up on total cost amounts to 89%. Different prices may be quoted to patients based on their personal circumstances – for example, if a particular patient is expected to require a longer than average stay in hospital after the operation, they will be quoted a higher price.

Denby maintains a risk register, and 5 key risks are highlighted: changing economic environment (in times of recession, unemployment increases and so there are less people covered by private health insurance); competition (there are 2 large competitors in Keeland); staffing (providing clinical excellence requires experienced and competent staff); clinical risk (i.e. the potential damage to reputation of clinical negligence); and political risk (a change in government policy may see revenue from KHS referrals decline).

Financial information

Denby has enjoyed growth in revenue of 6.4% in 2018, although income from both foreign and KHS referrals both declined compared to 2017. Operating profit grew by 35.8%. The group paid a dividend of K$23m in respect of 2018, which represented 57.5% of that year's earnings.

At the latest year end, 31 December 2018, Denby had $93m of cash and a gearing ratio (defined as debt/debt+equity) of 32.5%.

Comparable information is given for the market leader, Bronty Health Group, in the form of its latest financial statements, enabling a detailed comparison of the 2 companies' financial performance and position.

A share price graph is given showing how the company's share price has fared over the last 5 years. The most recent share price, of approximately $2.15 as at 1 March 2019, is considerably lower than its peak as at the start of 2017 when it stood at nearly $7.

3.2 Example tasks

In the real exam each task typically covers more than 1 assessment outcome, and can also cover more than 1 core activity. For simplicity we have taken 1 variant of the May 2019 exam and shown how this might represent core activities and assessment outcomes under the new syllabus.

Please note that not all core activities or associated assessment outcomes are covered; that is not possible due to differences with the old syllabus for strategic case study.

Answers are given at the back of the chapter.

<u>**Variant 1 – Task 1**</u>

B   Evaluate the business ecosystem and business environment

> *I can select and apply suitable strategic analytical tools.*

and

C   Recommend financing strategies

> *I can recommend suitable sources of finance.*

[Trigger]

Regina Chikaoanda, Denby's Chief Financial Officer, stops by your work space:

[Task]

"Please look at this proposal. Anthony Chan, our Medical Director, is keen to persuade the Board to support this venture. I need you to draft a paper for me that deals with two issues:

First of all, we will have to charge extremely high prices for treatment at the proposed centres in order to cover the cost of providing this level of care. How might we determine whether there would be sufficient demand?

Secondly, we will almost certainly have to borrow the funds needed to set up the Sports Injury Centres. Would it be irresponsible for Denby's Board to borrow the K$130 million required for this purpose?"

[Reference Material]

Proposal to establish sports injury clinics at Denby's Capital City Central and Northern City hospitals

Bardomaz has just launched a new type of ultrasound scanner. A skilled orthopaedic surgeon can use this equipment to assess damaged tissue in cases that would previously have required exploratory surgery to investigate properly. In many cases, a detailed scan will indicate that rest and physiotherapy will be sufficient to cure the injury, but the new scanner can also be used to enable microsurgery, again instead of traditional surgery.

It would cost K$50 million to buy one of these new scanners, to train a surgical team to use it to its full potential and to equip a microsurgery operating suite in the room so that any necessary surgery can be carried out immediately. It is unlikely that the KHS or any of our competitors will make that investment. So far, only two hospitals have acquired it and they are both located in Cornopia.

My proposal is quite ambitious. I propose that Denby should acquire two Bardomaz scanners, one for each of our Capital City Central and Northern City hospitals. Furthermore, we should add specialist physiotherapy suites that are staffed and equipped for managing sports injuries. We would promote these as "Denby Sports Injury Centres". Neither hospital would lose any of its existing facilities.

The new Sports Injury Centres would attract patients from a significant distance. Both cities have many major soccer teams located within a radius of 100 miles. Soccer players frequently suffer from tissue damage arising from wear and tear through training and playing. They also sustain injuries during matches and their employers are always keen to have the best possible treatment. Other professional sportspeople and wealthy amateur sports enthusiasts would be keen to have access to world-leading facilities to treat injuries that might otherwise curtail their playing careers. I believe that the market for these Centres could and would pay a high price for this standard of treatment.

I estimate the total investment, including the cost of the physiotherapy suites, at K$130 million. This is a great deal of money, but Denby has already developed an excellent reputation for the diagnosis and treatment of sporting injuries using more conventional techniques and we should aim to build on that.

Anthony Chan Medical Director

Exercise 1
Write your response to Regina Chikaoanda

Variant 1 – Task 2

A   Develop business strategy

I can evaluate strategic options (digital and otherwise)

I can recommend response to opportunities and threats arising from digital technologies

[Trigger]

A month has passed. The proposal to establish the Denby Sports Injury Centres is still being discussed. You receive the following email:

[Task]

From: **Regina Chikaoanda, Chief Financial Officer**

To: **Senior Manager Subject: Sports injuries**

Hi

I have attached a meeting note that I prepared after a discussion with Denby's Head of Orthopaedic Surgery concerning the creation of Denby Sports Injury Centres (DSICs). I need you to draft a briefing paper concerning two issues that follow on from this meeting:

Firstly, should we regard the intellectual property in the form of knowledge and experience developed by our orthopaedic surgeons as a strategic resource that should be protected and preserved?

Secondly, would it be possible to develop an information system that would preserve and share this intellectual knowledge electronically, *even* if Dr Mtimbe's concerns with regard to DSIC prove correct?

Regina

[Reference Material]

Meeting note

Present: Dr Alexander Mtimbe, Head of Orthopaedic Surgery; Anthony Chan, Medical Director; Regina Chikaoanda, Chief Financial Officer

We met at Dr Mtimbe's request, to discuss his concerns arising from the proposal to create two "Denby Sports Injury Centres" (DSICs). Dr Mtimbe pointed out that all of Denby's hospitals have orthopaedic surgery departments, man y of which are regarded as the best facilities in their respective regions for treating sports injuries. All have experience of treating professional sportspeople, including leading soccer players, who often suffer severe injuries.

Dr Mtimbe believes that the doctors, nurses and physiotherapists who presently work in Denby's orthopaedic surgery departments benefit from treating a wide range of patients. Treating highly paid and important sportspeople develops skills that can then be applied to the treatment of other patients. He is concerned that this opportunity will be lost because there will only be two DSICs, which will attract most professional sportspeople away from Denby's other hospitals.

Such technically challenging cases also encourage dialogue between medical staff both within the orthopaedic surgery departments responsible for these patients and between hospitals. Sportspeople always need to make the fullest possible recovery in the shortest possible time and that often forces orthopaedic surgeons to consider slightly unorthodox treatment plans. These provide a strong incentive for senior doctors to consult, both to share experience and also to reduce Denby's liability in the event that the treatment does not work.

Again, that dialogue has created a body of intellectual property that enables Denby to remain at the forefront of orthopaedic surgery. Dr Mtimbe believes that the staff assigned to the DSICs will be too busy with their own patient loads to consult with colleagues from outside the DSICs.

Dr Mtimbe believes that the creation of DSIC will undermine the strength of orthopaedic surgery across Denby.

It was agreed that Dr Mtimbe's concerns would be considered by Denby's Board before any final decision was reached concerning DSIC.

Exercise 2

Write your response to Regina Chikaoanda

Variant 1 – Task 3

B   Evaluate the business ecosystem and business environment

I can recommend responses to economic, political and currency risks

and

C   Recommend financing strategies

I can recommend and apply business valuation models

[Trigger]

A further two months have passed. Denby's Board has agreed to acquire the new scanning equipment and to create two "Denby Sports Injury Centres" (D SICs). You have been asked to attend a special meeting of Denby's Board, in an advisory capacity:

[Task]

John Jenkins, CEO (in the chair)	I have tabled copies of the letter of intent that was couriered to Bardomaz this morning. They insisted on us paying in their home currency. The present exchange rate is C$2.00 = K$1.00, so this will cost us K$100 million.
Regina Chikaoanda, CFO	I am nervous about the potential currency loss on the balancing payment of C$180 million. I think that we need to hedge.
John Jenkins, CEO	I disagree, Regina. Firstly, Cornopia's inflation and interest rates are higher than Keeland's, so the C$ will weaken against the K$, which will make it cheaper to settle the C$180 million balance in nine months. Secondly, I intend to borrow the C$180 million from a Cornopian bank, repayable with fixed interest, over 15 years. That will eliminate any currency risk associated with acquiring and paying for this equipment.
Regina Chikaoanda, CFO *(Turning to you)*	Please evaluate John's arguments with respect to the weakening of the C$ against the K$ exchange rate over the next nine months, and also his argument that arranging a C$180 million fixed rate loan from a Cornopian Bank will eliminate the impact of currency movements.
Robert Borr, Commercial Director *(Turning to you)*	I would also like you to discuss the implications of this project for Denby's share price and whether extending our integrated reporting would help to avoid a fall in share price.

[Reference Material]

Mr Luis Gonzales

Sales Director

Bardomaz

Millennium City

Cornopia

Dear Luis

Letter of Intent

I am writing to express our intention to place a formal offer for two BardomazExplorer systems. You will install one machine at Denby's Capital City Central Hospital and the other at our Northern City Hospital. You will provide two of our surgical teams with full training in the safe and efficient use of this equipment.

We will pay C$200 million for the equipment and all associated costs of delivery, installation and training. We will make an initial payment of C$20 million when we place a formal order, with the remainder on delivery in nine months' time.

Yours sincerely,

John Jenkins

Chief Executive Officer

 Exercise 3

Write your response to Regina Chikaoanda and Robert Borr

Next steps:

(1)   You can begin to revisit and revise technical material from your previous studies according to the core activities and assessment outcomes given in this chapter. However we suggest you continue to do this alongside working through the rest of this book so you can also learn how you may need to apply the knowledge.

(2)   Remember that you will not be required to perform calculations in the case study exam. However you may need to explain or interpret calculations and so an appreciation of how they are prepared is still relevant and useful. You will also receive credit for any relevant calculations that you choose to produce and interpret in answering a task

(3)   In the following chapters we do a complete walkthrough of the prototype sample paper issued in June 2019.

4   Solutions to chapter exercises

Exercise 1

Requirement 1 – demand for sports injury clinics

From Anthony's description, the scanner will offer advantages in terms of speed of recovery from injuries, but will not necessarily cure problems that were previously untreatable. The treatment will have a relatively narrow market in terms of patients who are both willing and able to pay for faster recovery. There is unlikely to be a mass market for this type of treatment. As a starting point, Denby should approach potential buyers, with a view to establishing whether they would be likely to use this service. If their initial response is that they would have little or no need for such an expensive service then Denby should probably regard that as a strong argument not to proceed.

Anthony seems to regard professional soccer clubs as potential clients. The loss of a key player through injury could put a club under significant pressure, both sporting and financial, and so it would be worth establishing whether they would be interested in Denby acquiring this capability. The approach would have to be framed carefully because the clubs are unlikely to make any binding commitment to use this equipment, even if they argue that Denby should acquire it. They could be positive about the principle of Denby making the investment and may then continue to use conventional treatments or fly their players to Cornopia if they require treatment.

Denby needs to conduct a more thorough analysis to determine whether the clubs would have a meaningful incentive to pay for the treatment that could be provided by the new technology, even if that is simply a check on the credibility of any comments made by the clubs.

Denby should start by making contact with major soccer clubs' doctors and physiotherapists in order to discuss the numbers of players who have been injured in recent years. If there are actually very few injuries then that might suggest that there is very little real demand from soccer clubs. If there have been more injuries then the next step is to establish whether the clubs might have used the new technology if it had been available. Denby could ask to discuss case histories of injured players, including prognosis before treatment, the actual outcome and whether the availability of the proposed new technology would have helped. The club could then be asked whether the players were sufficiently valuable to have justified the cost of treatment using ultrasound and microsurgery in order to establish how many referrals each major club might have made on, say, an annual basis.

Denby also has records relating to sports injury patients whom it has treated using conventional means. These records could be studied with a view to determining the number of cases in which the new technology would have had a beneficial clinical effect. Denby could then estimate the net additional cost of using the proposed new equipment compared to the patients' actual billings and also the difference in terms of the outcome of that treatment. Denby could then have identified patients who would have benefitted significantly and could ask them whether they would have paid that additional fee in order to have had that additional expected benefit. It would be ideal if Denby could link the net additional cost to any economic information that the company has about these patients. A professional golfer, say, might be prepared to invest a month's income in securing a more rapid recovery from an injury. It is unlikely that many patients would be willing or able to spend, say, a year's income.

Requirement 2 – borrowing

Borrowing an additional K$130m would increase Denby's gearing from 550/(550 + 1,144) = 32% to (550 + 130)/(550 + 130 + 1,144) = 37%. That is quite a significant increase in gearing, so Denby could find that it is getting close to gearing restrictions in any covenants on existing borrowings. It could also find that the increase causes shareholders some concerns about whether Denby is borrowing too aggressively to fund this project. It probably would be irresponsible for Denby to allow itself to get close to its maximum borrowing capacity or to borrow to the point where the share price starts to fall.

The additional funding will be invested in specialised medical equipment, in modifying physiotherapy suites, and similar costs. Those assets are unlikely to provide the lender with any meaningful security. In the event that Denby becomes unable to service the loan then the assets will undoubtedly have to be sold at a discount. That could mean that Denby is forced to liquidate assets associated to existing, and profitable, areas of the business in the event that the new sports centres fail. The lenders will possibly wish to take security against other assets in any case because they will not be interested in having the right to repossess assets that will have little or no market for resale. Borrowing in this manner will expose other areas of the company to the risks of default and so it may be regarded as a rather reckless thing to do.

Denby's cost of debt, ignoring tax relief, is 22/550 = 4%, so the additional borrowing would increase reduce profit before tax by 130 × 4% = K$5.2 million. That decrease would represent a significant proportion of profit before tax and would be a further argument that the borrowing could be regarded as reckless. The additional finance charge should be considered in the further context of the fixed costs associated with staffing and depreciation of the new equipment. Combining the borrowing costs with the additional expenses will create a significant risk that profits will fall, with an even greater decrease on return on capital employed.

The speculative nature of this project will introduce a speculative element into Denby's revenues and operating profit. That suggests that it would be more prudent to reduce gearing by raising funding from equity. Higher gearing will accentuate any volatility created by the new venture which appears to be a highly volatile proposal. At the very least, Denby should consider its forecast revenues and operating profits and should revisit the gearing decision on the basis of a prudent analysis of the business case.

Examiners comments

Requirement 1 – Demand for sports injury clinics

Candidates should have drawn on the relevant facts that were stated in the scenario, and also trailed to some extent in the pre-seen material. Denby has considerable expertise in treating orthopaedic injuries, but this new venture is intended as a much more ambitious offering that will rely on finding patients who are prepared to pay a considerable premium for a more speedy or more certain recovery.

Marks were awarded for any sensible suggestions as to how demand for this service might be forecast. Stronger candidates might be realistic about some of the difficulties arising from the fact that potential patients/clients have little to lose from claiming that they would use this service and then making alternative arrangements. Answers were not very strong for this requirement. Candidates should have discussed research into possible demand. They could have asked local sports clubs what they thought for example.

They could have sent out surveys or had an interesting website which could have asked about the likelihood of readers using the service. These results could have been examined and used to forecast demand. A number of candidates answered another question which was the reasons why the service would be popular, few marks were awarded for this approach.

Requirement 2 – Borrowing

The question essentially raised two related issues. Borrowing to fund this project will increase gearing. That raises questions about whether the gearing ratio is likely to be increased beyond acceptable limits. Better candidates should have recognised that gearing will increase, but not to the extent that there is a categorical argument that it has become excessive.

The increase in gearing should have been considered against the possibility that the new venture will have an adverse effect on operating profit. It should always be recognised that high gearing is a problem because it intensifies the effect of volatility in operating profit on the profit for the year. If there is no volatility in operating profit then gearing is much less of an issue.

Candidates might also have considered whether lenders would be prepared to accept Denby's assets as security. They may have limited resale value, if a lender could accept the bad publicity associated with foreclosing on a hospital and removing potentially life- saving equipment. This question was done quite well by many candidates with many discussing gearing well. Weaker candidates did

Exercise 2

Requirement 1 – intellectual property

At present, all of Denby's hospitals provide orthopaedic care. This creates a need to attract patients to buy those services. Some patients may be attracted to Denby because they require surgery and do not wish to wait for KHS treatment or are prepared to pay more for the greater comfort and privacy associated with private healthcare. Those patients may not be particularly interested in the expertise of Denby's doctors. They may simply assume that all practising doctors are competent. Straightforward injuries and medical problems that are to be treated by established techniques will probably require little or nothing in the way of consultation between doctors.

Dr Mtimbe's arguments concerning sports injuries do make sense. Sports professionals' careers may depend on making a full and rapid recovery and that may provide an incentive for orthopaedic surgeons to learn and apply the latest developments. The risks of doing so are potentially high, partly because of the ethical risk associated with harming a patient and partly because of the costs and adverse publicity associated with causing further problems. Soccer players and their clubs may be unwilling to take a risk with a proposed treatment unless Denby can claim that it has a successful track record. Developing a list of techniques in which Denby has experienced staff will enable the company to attract more high-profile patients.

There could be a strategic benefit in spreading orthopaedic services across all hospitals. It will, for example, ensure that there is more widespread adoption of the latest techniques into mainstream medicine. Even if patients are not particularly concerned with being treated with the latest techniques, if Denby can help patients recover more quickly and more consistently then it will save costs in the process. Consultation will reduce the potential costs associated with paying damages and adverse publicity because it will be more difficult for a patient to accuse the company of negligence in the event that they do not recover as hoped. Sharing experience will also enable Denby to roll out any new technologies when their costs decrease to the point where they can be used more widely. That could assist Denby to obtain a commercial advantage over the other private hospitals.

It may prove difficult for Denby to safeguard any intellectual property that it creates, thereby reducing its value as a strategic resource. For example, if the DSICs leave Denby with a small number of orthopaedic surgeons who have valuable expertise then Denby's competitors may be tempted to lure them away. Competitors may offer to enhance salaries. They may also be able to offer even more advanced equipment or other desirable benefits that Denby could struggle to compete with. Concentrating advanced skills in the DSICs might also discourage the sharing of knowledge and experience, making the loss of senior doctors even more serious. There will be fewer really senior doctors and so they will be less willing to encourage their colleagues from other hospitals to seek advice. Furthermore, Denby may be unable to prevent its doctors from sharing knowledge with doctors from competing private hospitals.

Medical ethics may forbid doctors from refusing to offer advice when it has been specifically requested.

Requirement 2 – information system

It would be difficult to design a reliable information system that enabled doctors to share their experiences and consult one another in a meaningful way. Dr Mtimbe's point seems to be that doctors often need to consult colleagues because cases differ to a significant extent. For example, the effects of a particular treatment could be affected by the severity of the injury or other aspects of the patient's medical history and so a database that links treatments to situations may not reduce the need for communication between doctors. Such an information system might make it easier to identify colleagues with relevant experience, but it would not necessarily make the relevant information accessible in the manner implied by Regina. Encouraging doctors to seek consultations with colleagues could lead to an inefficient use of time, with constant interruptions. Also, some decisions have to be taken quickly and surgeons are not always available to offer advice when crucial decisions have to be made because, say, they are operating.

The information system will not be as adaptable as direct consultations between experienced doctors. For example, it could be discovered that an accepted treatment carries previously unrecognised risks in certain circumstances. The information system may not make those risks apparent in files relating to cases that had a successful outcome, because the patient could have recovered despite the risks. It is unlikely that the doctors would have followed the advice from the information system blindly in any case, but they will have to consider whether their colleagues were aware of the latest knowledge when they input their cases into the system. Doctors may be reluctant to base decisions on the system if it starts to introduce further complications into reading and interpreting the output.

There could be a significant cost in terms of time and effort to input details into the information system. It will only have value if doctors can establish whether past cases that have been highlighted by the system are relevant to the cases for which they are seeking a consultation. The records will have to be comprehensive to allow for meaningful comparisons between cases on factors such as prior medical history. If doctors resent this inconvenience then they may not give a full account of their cases, potentially undermining the value of the system.

It may be unnecessary to create a separate information system given that Denby will already have detailed medical records online. It may be possible to use Big Data analytics to gather useful insights from existing patient records. One advantage is that the data will be open to re-evaluation in the event that, say, a particular drug is found to have side effects in a particular situation. The system would also reduce the risk that the findings could be biased by anecdotal evidence. For example, a doctor could prescribe a particular drug and believe that it cured the patient when the patient was actually recovering anyway. Big Data analytics would be able to identify whether there was statistical evidence to support the use of a drug in a particular situation. The application of Big Data analytics in these circumstances would, of course, be an information system even if it took a different form from that envisaged by Regina.

Examiners comments

Requirement 1 – Intellectual property

Candidates should probably have considered both sides of this argument, because it is relatively complex.

Denby is in competition with other private hospitals and is also, to an extent, competing for patients' willingness to pay for treatment that would otherwise be provided for free by the KHS. Any form of expertise and skill that the company's doctors can apply to the treatment of patients has the potential to increase revenues.

Better answers should have reflected the fact that medical ethics might make it difficult to withhold information from other hospitals, even if they are in competition with Denby for private patients. Similarly, the doctors themselves are free to leave and it would undoubtedly be impossible to prevent them from drawing on the experience and expertise they developed while working at Denby.

There were some good answers to this requirement. Generally most candidates managed to write something sensible for this requirement.

Requirement 2 – Information system

The pre-seen material highlights some of the complexities of treating patients. Candidates should have recognised that it would be difficult to develop an information gathering system that offered even a fraction of the flexibility associated with a consultation between two or more professional doctors. No two cases are exactly the same and so a database that logs the success or failure of treatment plans will only be of any use if it captures every potentially relevant factor.

Candidates could have seen this as an opportunity to draw upon Big Data Analytics in order to offer an alternative to a traditional information system. It was not, however, mandatory to do so in order to earn full marks.

Very few candidates discussed Big Data in their answers.

Answers to this requirement were surprisingly weak, few candidates seemed to have a good idea what would be involved in developing a good system. Many candidates just achieved a passing score. It was a lack of application and a lack of knowledge which led to lower marks.

Exercise 3

Requirement 1 – exchange rate and foreign currency borrowing

The economic indicators do suggest that the C$ can be expected to weaken against the K$. Purchasing Power Parity Theory suggests that the real cost of goods will be the same regardless of currency. That suggests that a currency that is subject to a high rate of inflation will tend to weaken in order to offset its diminishing purchasing power. Similarly, the International Fisher Effect suggests that the same real rate of interest will be charged on any given currency. Again, that suggests that the C$ will decline against the K$ to compensate for the difference in the interest rates.

John's arguments make sense from a theoretical perspective, but there can be no guarantee that these theories will eliminate the risks. There is empirical evidence to suggest that Purchasing Power Parity Theory and the International Fisher Effect can provide an accurate indication of the direction of any currency change, but they do not offer a precise and accurate forecast of future rates.

Given that the outstanding balance will be C$180m, even a relatively small forecasting error could lead to a significant variation in the amount payable. It is even possible that the Cornopian Government will act to maintain and protect the value of its currency over a relatively short period, such as the nine months that is the case here, and so Denby could suffer a significant additional cost.

Arranging to borrow C$180m will have the effect of hedging the lump sum payment that is due in nine months. Once the loan has been arranged, the lender will settle the amount outstanding as at the due date in full, regardless of any changes in currency values. Given that there is a large balance due and also a potential concern arising from the economic indicators that suggest a currency movement could be forthcoming, it might be prudent to hedge by borrowing in this way. Unfortunately, it will then leave Denby with a commitment to repay the loan with interest over the next 15 years.

Settling the loan will expose Denby to movements between C$ and K$ for an extended period. The interest rate on the loan is fixed, so the C$ payments are known and will be payable over the next 15 years. During that time, there could be significant movements, both strengthening and weakening of the C$. The fact that the lender agreed to a fixed rate loan suggests that the lender anticipates that the C$ will strengthen, which would be associated with a reduction in the C$ interest rate. The only consolation is that the payments extend into the long-term future and so the payments have a low net present value and the additional cost will not start to affect shareholder wealth for some time.

Requirement 2 – share price

The implications for the share price will depend in part on the extent to which the markets believe that this will be a positive NPV investment. In the short term, the announcement of the project will have to be evaluated by the shareholders and they will form an opinion as to whether the investment makes commercial sense. Hopefully, they will be encouraged by the fact that it will give Denby an advantage in competing for the custom of major soccer clubs and professional sports people. Presumably, Denby will make a public announcement of this new service and will describe its advantages, if only to ensure that potential patients are aware of it. That will help the shareholders understand the value of the investment.

This could be regarded as a risky investment, but the shareholders should hold diversified portfolios and so will only be concerned with the systematic risk of the venture. The factors that will affect the success or failure of the DSICs are unlikely to be influenced by factors that affect the stock market as a whole. Their required rate of return may well be lower than that used by the directors in evaluating this project and so the share price may be more likely to increase than decrease. There is, however, always a danger that the shareholders will be concerned that the directors have taken an unacceptable risk or have decided to invest in the project for selfish reasons that could decrease the market value.

Integrated reporting would give the shareholders additional insights into the value creation process. That should make it easier for them to understand the project from the directors' point of view. The shareholders are more likely to share the directors' optimism if the board clarifies the reasoning behind investing in this project. The integrated report should clearly describe the strategic focus and should look more to the future. Such an emphasis will make the board's logic more apparent to the shareholders. A clear explanation of how the centres will fit into Denby's overall strategy will give the shareholders a clearer basis for evaluating and supporting the board's expectations and will, hopefully, enable them to better understand the project's strategic fit.

The integrated report will add to the usual reporting of historical capitals. Giving the shareholders insights into the manufactured capitals will enable them to better understand the new technology and how it will enable the two centres to treat patients more effectively. It will also make it clearer how this technology will assist Denby to compete in this market against other private hospitals. The integrated report will also highlight the impact that the investment will have on intellectual capital, stressing the experience that using this equipment will provide. It will also provide insights into social capital, including the extent to which this project will help Denby develop closer ties to the management of major soccer clubs.

Examiners comments

This section is essentially two pairs of linked requirements. They are presented as two pairs in the question paper, but the answers are shown separately below for the sake of simplifying the marking grid.

Requirement 1 – Exchange rate

The first part of this requirement deals with the PPP theory and the question of whether it might be cheaper to borrow in a foreign currency that might decrease in value.

Candidates should have been able to explain the theory behind this model, as well as indicating some understanding of the empirical evidence concerning its effectiveness in practice. The fact that the model does not work exactly as the mathematics suggest leaves some scope for risk.

There were many very good answers to this question.

Requirement 2 – Foreign currency borrowing

This part effectively asks candidates to consider whether natural hedging might be of value in this scenario. Better candidates will recognise that the timings of the cash flows will disrupt the hedging. This requirement was performed badly with many candidates showing very poor knowledge of this part of the syllabus. Few candidates gave reasonable answers to this requirement. This was mainly due to lack of knowledge.

Requirement 3 – Share price

Candidates may preface their answers with a reference to the Efficient Market Hypothesis (EMH), although that should not have been a major part of this answer.

Better candidates viewed the impact on the share price in terms of the information that is available for the market to process and the extent to which the shareholders agree that this is a sound investment. Weaker candidates were unable to really answer this requirement and offered no more than a surface discussion of EMH. Again, knowledge of this part of the syllabus was surprisingly weak.

Requirement 4 – Integrated reporting

Candidates should know what integrated reporting is, but a detailed description of what it is was not worth many marks unless the description was tied back to the scenario. Few candidates could do much more than briefly mention the six capitals and say integrated reporting was a good idea. Marks were close to the passing score with few high marks being awarded. Candidates knew the theory of integrated reporting but poor at application to the case.

May and August 2020 real exam – pre-seen information

1   Introduction

The Case Study Examinations are like no other CIMA exam; there is no new syllabus to study or formulae to learn. The best way to be successful at this level is to practise using past case study exams and mock exams based on your real live case study. By reviewing previous case studies alongside your current case you will improve your commercial thought processes and will be more aware of what the examiner expects. By sitting mock exams, under timed conditions you can hone your exam techniques and, in particular, your time management skills.

This textbook is therefore based on this principle. It presents the real case study exam from May and August 2020, and uses this to demonstrate the skills and techniques that you must master to be successful. This case, Runnabout, will be used to walkthrough the processes and approach. The remainder of this chapter contains the Runnabout pre-seen material.

We would advise that you skim read this now before moving on to Chapter 4 where you will be provided with more guidance on how to familiarise yourself with the pre-seen material.

Strategic case study exam – May/August 2020 exam – pre-seen materials

Contents

Introduction

You are a senior manager in the finance function at Runnabout, the parent company of the Runnabout Group. You report directly to the Board and advise on special projects and strategic matters.

Runnabout is a quoted company that operates pay-as-you go "hoverboard" vehicles for use by the public in major cities. Geeland is a large and prosperous country with a population of more than one billion people. Geeland's major cities have grown rapidly and many are struggling with the difficulties caused by traffic congestion and the resulting pollution.

Runnabout is based in Geeland where the currency is the G$. Geeland requires companies to prepare their financial statements in accordance with International Financial Reporting Standards (IFRS).

Geeland has an active and well-regulated stock exchange. Companies that are quoted on the exchange are required to adhere to the Geeland Code of Corporate Governance, which sets out detailed regulations relating to the governance arrangements for quoted companies.

The micromobility industry

Micromobility is a relatively recent innovation, dating from the early 2000s. It involves the provision of one-way rental services that enable users to complete the so-called "last mile" of a journey quickly and efficiently. Micromobility users rent, say, a bicycle, scooter or hoverboard from one location and return it to another location that is conveniently close to their final destination. Typically, users are commuters who need a fast and efficient way to get from, say, a city-centre railway station to their offices.

Micromobility is generally used for relatively short journeys and so augments traditional public transport rather than replacing it. Commuters might be encouraged to travel into the city centre by train or bus, knowing that micromobility solutions are available enables them to get to work on time, without walking long distances or relying on local bus or taxi services that are likely to be slow-moving because of rush hour traffic.

Bicycle-sharing

Bicycle-sharing permits users who are registered with a provider to rent bicycles on a short-term basis. The provider creates a network of bicycle docking  stations or "docks" across a suitable location such as a city centre. Users can release a bicycle from a dock by identifying themselves, usually by swiping a debit or credit card. They can use the bicycle for as long as they wish but are charged a hire fee from releasing the bicycle until it is returned to one of the provider's docks, which may not be the dock from which the bicycle was taken. Providers locate docks in places which encourage one-way journeys. For example, city centre bus and railway stations make convenient pickup points for morning commuters. Docks close to major office buildings are convenient dropping off points. Users may then, if they wish, hire a bicycle for the first part of their return journey, taking a bicycle from a dock close to their place of employment and dropping it off at the station from which they will catch their bus or train home.

Bicycle-sharing is a relatively cheap and convenient way to cover the so-called "last mile" of a journey to a city-centre location. Cycling is generally faster than walking and can also be faster than a local bus service when rush-hour traffic is taken into account. Bicycle hire charges for sharing schemes are generally inexpensive.

While peak demand for bicycles occurs during the morning and evening rush hours, there is a constant demand throughout the day and late into the evening. Students often use bicycle-sharing schemes to travel between their accommodation and their college campuses. Tourists find them useful to explore cities and for transportation between attractions such as museums. Many cities have large numbers of flat-dwellers who live within a few miles of the city centre and who find it convenient to be able to use a bicycle sharing-scheme to get to and from work and for short journeys outside of work.

Bicycle-sharing schemes came into being in the early 2000s. They have since grown and developed in many cities around the world. There has been some controversy about their use and they have also been subject to competition from other types of transportation.

It is generally illegal to ride bicycles on pavements or in pedestrianised areas. Most countries' laws require cyclists to ride on designated bicycle lanes or on the roads when bicycle lanes are not available. Not surprisingly, increasing the numbers of cyclists on the roads increases the numbers of injuries involving cyclists.

Strict legislation has been introduced to reduce the risks associated with riding bicycles owned by sharing schemes. Operators must ensure that bicycles are roadworthy. Most operators require users to return a bicycle to its dock immediately if they believe that it is defective and to inform the operator of the bicycle's status using an app, in which case the bicycle will not be released to another user. Operators generally employ mechanics who attend to simple repairs such as flat tyres while the bicycle is still in its dock. For more serious repairs, the bicycles are transported to the operator's depot by van.

In many countries, including Geeland, cyclists are required to wear crash helmets. Bicycle-sharing schemes have no specific responsibility for ensuring that cyclists comply with this law, but it does mean that scheme users must either purchase and carry helmets if they wish to hire a bicycle or they must risk being stopped by the police and fined for failing to wear a helmet.

Bicycle sharing schemes continue to be popular in many countries and the number of trips made by users of those schemes is increasing steadily. There are, however, some competing modes of transport in this market:

Electric bicycles		Electric bicycles have battery powered motors that augment the users' pedalling and so require less effort. Many commuters prefer to use electric bicycles because of this. The bicycles' batteries are automatically recharged while they are in the docking station.

Electric scooters		Electric scooters are powered by batteries. They do not require any effort from their users. They are recharged while docked. They have proved controversial because they are often ridden on pavements rather than on the road and have been involved in accidents involving pedestrians.
Hoverboards		Hoverboards are generally ridden on pavements in a city context. They can be recharged while docked and used in a similar manner to electric scooters. Hoverboards are slower than electric scooters.

Hoverboard-sharing

Hoverboards do not actually "hover". They are two-wheeled vehicles that are  driven by electric motors, powered by rechargeable batteries. The user stands on a platform that fits between the two wheels. The hoverboard is controlled by the operator leaning in the desired direction of travel. A slight lean forward makes the machine roll ahead and leaning to the left or right makes the machine turn in that direction. Leaning backward will make the hoverboard slow down and reverse if the operator continues to lean in that direction after stopping.

Hoverboards, which are sometimes referred to as "self-balancing scooters" work as follows:

Electric motors		Computer
Each wheel is powered by its own electric motor, which enables the hoverboard to steer. If the user wishes to turn left then the right-hand wheel spins a little faster, making the board turn left. The motors also prevent the board from tilting by more than a few degrees, even when it is standing still.		The electric motors are controlled by an onboard computer that is programmed to manage both stability and movement. Sensors in the platform provide the computer with inputs that keep the platform stable enough to stand on and that detect the user's control inputs to control speed and direction.
Gyroscope	**Platform**	**Battery**
A gyroscope built into the platform enables the computer to measure the angle of the platform. The computer sends instructions to the wheels using feedback from the gyroscope to prevent the platform from tilting.	The platform is strong enough to carry the weight of the user. It carries the hoverboard's other components. It also contains pressure switches that measure the control inputs from the user.	Hoverboards generally use 36-volt batteries, which provide sufficient power to ensure a satisfactory performance. The hoverboard's range is determined by the capacity of the batteries.

Hoverboards come in different sizes, depending on whether they are being sold as adult transportation or children's toys. Adult hoverboards can reach speeds of approximately 10 miles per hour (or 16 kilometres per hour), although riding at full speed will quickly run down the battery. A fully-charged hoverboard that is driven at the equivalent of a brisk walking pace can travel over 15 miles (or 24 kilometres) before running out of power.

Hoverboards trace their roots back to the launch of self-balancing scooters in the early 2000s. They captured the public's attention because they looked inherently unstable and yet they could be ridden with apparent ease because of a combination of ingenious engineering and electronics.

Early hoverboards were too expensive for consumers to buy, but they quickly became established as a means of fast and efficient transportation for staff who needed to be mobile within areas populated by pedestrians. For example, security staff in theme parks, shopping malls and airports can respond to alerts quickly without having to rely on conventional vehicles that would be too large and could pose an unacceptable risk to the public. These hoverboards also enable the rider to see over pedestrians because the platform is a few inches above ground level. The hoverboards have other uses, such as giving first aiders and paramedics the ability to get to a casualty quickly or giving staff supervisors the ability to attend incidents or interact with staff spread across their areas of responsibility.

The machines themselves require no training to operate. The rider simply must lean in the desired direction of travel and can regulate speed by leaning more to go faster and less to slow down. These machines are not, however, without their risks, especially if they are operated irresponsibly. They can generally travel faster than a brisk walking pace, so the rider may have to navigate around pedestrians. The user could fall off or strike an obstacle if riding carelessly and a collision with a pedestrian would be potentially serious because the combined mass of the hoverboard and its user would have significant momentum when travelling at speed.

Hoverboards are generally designed to operate on smooth surfaces, such as pavements and tiled floors. They cannot be ridden safely on roads because their wheels could catch in potholes and drains. They would also be vulnerable to motor vehicles and would force passing cyclists away from the kerb and into the paths of larger and faster vehicles.

Hoverboards have also raised safety risks associated with their batteries overheating and bursting into flames. Hoverboards require both high voltages and high currents in order to ensure that the platform remains stable and achieves an acceptable speed. Loose connections can result in a short circuit that causes the battery to overheat and possibly catch fire. In extreme cases, rough handling of a battery can crack the battery's case, creating the risk of an explosion if the electrolyte is released and comes into contact with the air.

Batteries are vulnerable to damage if hoverboards are ridden carelessly or if they are mistreated in use or storage.

Runnabout

Runnabout was established in 2005. The company was created to rent bicycles in response to the successful launch of city centre bicycle-sharing schemes that had been launched in several other countries. The company started with three docks in the centre of Geeland's Capital City. It rapidly expanded until it had a total of 32 docks across Capital City and a significant presence in 14 other cities across the country.

Runnabout was quoted on the Geeland Stock Exchange in 2010.

In 2012, Runnabout's Board commissioned a strategic review of the market for micromobility in Geeland. The directors were concerned that demand for sharing schemes based on conventional bicycles was tailing off because commuters were becoming unwilling to rely on pedal power for even short distances. Geeland is a relatively flat country, so cyclists do not have to contend with many hills, but the weather can be rather windy, which can make cycling quite tiring.

On an experimental basis, Runnabout modified some of the docks in Capital City to operate both electric and conventional bicycles. That enabled users to choose between pedal driven and electric bicycles, with a slightly higher rental fee for electric bicycles to cover the cost of recharging batteries. The docks were located to enable users to use electric bicycles on frequently used routes. Runnabout also replaced all of the docks and bicycles in Western City so that users could use electric bicycles across the whole of that city's network. Runnabout found that the introduction of electric bicycles did little to stimulate demand.

In 2014, the government of Geeland introduced legislation to make it mandatory to wear helmets while cycling. That reduced demand for both pedal driven and electric bicycles. The company experimented with various schemes, such as offering to sell scheme members helmets at discounted prices.

The new helmet legislation coincided with the launch of two competing bicycle-sharing schemes in Geeland. Both of Runnabout's new competitors focussed their attention on Capital City, but soon started to expand into other towns and cities. These competitors grew steadily.

In 2016, Runnabout replaced its bicycles with hoverboards in Western City. The docks that had previously been used to secure bicycles were replaced with hoverboard-compatible docks. These were an immediate success, with hoverboards quickly becoming popular with many commuters because they required even less effort to ride than electric bicycles. They also opened up new markets, with hoverboards proving popular with tourists, who found them an ideal way to explore a city, either individually or as part of a guided tour. They are particularly suitable for tours of seafronts in coastal resorts because they are generally flat and offer wide paved areas that are free of traffic. Hoverboards also proved popular with shoppers, who could park at the edge of a city centre and use a hoverboard to get to the shops. Runnabout was encouraged by these results and so replaced bicycles with hoverboards across Geeland.

Runnabout moved quickly to establish its hoverboard-sharing scheme in Capital City and in each of the other 14 cities in which it previously operated as a bicycle-sharing operator. The other bicycle-sharing companies continue to rent out both pedal and electric bicycles, but none have expressed any interest in converting to hoverboards or other forms of micromobility. The city authorities have made it clear that they wish to observe the effects of hoverboards on the flow of pedestrians and traffic in city streets and also on the safety implications of these devices. Each of the 15 cities in which Runnabout operates (including Capital City) has announced that it will not permit any other hoverboard-sharing schemes on its streets, leaving Runnabout as the sole provider for the foreseeable future. All of those cities will, however, continue to encourage the development of bicycle sharing.

In Geeland, the responsibility for the management of road and pedestrian safety is a matter for individual town and city councils (the elected local government authorities responsible for many services including transport). Companies that wish to offer any form of public transport, including micromobility services, must be licensed by the appropriate town or city council.

Runnabout employs 15,000 people, including 2,000 planning and analysis staff at its Head Office. The company's experience of providing micromobility services has given it a deep understanding of the flow of pedestrians through city centres. That understanding extends to the interaction between micromobility and different forms of public transport, to the extent that town and city councils have sought advice about transportation services from Runnabout on a consultancy basis.

Runnabout has a total of 30,270,000 registered users. Registration requires the user to create an account on Runnabout's secure website and to download a mobile phone app. Registration is free, but all hoverboard rides are charged to the user's credit card. When creating an account, users must provide their 16-digit credit card number accompanied by their 3-digit credit card validation (CCV) number.

Users can use the app to locate the nearest Runnabout dock that has available

hoverboards. Alternatively, users can walk to convenient docks in the hope that there will be sufficient hoverboards available. Each dock has a 4-digit location number. Each user logs into the app using an individual pin number and then inputs the location number of the dock from which they wish to hire a hoverboard.

Runnabout's central server verifies the user's account and sends a 5-digit one-time code to the user's phone. The user keys the one-time code into the dock and the dock releases a hoverboard.

The app can locate nearby docks to which a hoverboard can be returned, or the user can simply ride to a known dock. The user activates the dock using the phone app and is directed to place the hoverboard in a bay at street level. That brings the hire period to an end and the cost is charged to the user's credit card.

The mechanism inside the dock interrogates the electronic self-diagnosis software on the hoverboard's computer. The hoverboard is taken out of service and is set aside for collection by a mechanic if it reports any mechanical or electrical failures. Otherwise, it is docked and charged ready for hire by the next user.

Runnabout's mechanics must collect and relocate hoverboards throughout the day in response to capacity in the docks and availability of hoverboards. On a typical weekday, 43% of all hoverboard hires occur during the "rush hour" periods of 7.00 to 9.00am and 4.00 to 6.00 pm. During the morning rush hour, many hoverboards are undocked from bus and railway stations and redocked in city centre locations close to places of employment. The opposite is true of the evening rush hour. Runnabout uses vans to relocate hoverboards from docks that are close to being full up to docks that are in danger of running out of hoverboards. That ensures that users can rely on finding an available hoverboard that can be redocked close to their final destination. Runnabout's vans also uplift faulty hoverboards for repair.

The average hire period for one of Runnabout's hoverboards is 22 minutes. The revenue and cost associated with a typical hire is as follows:

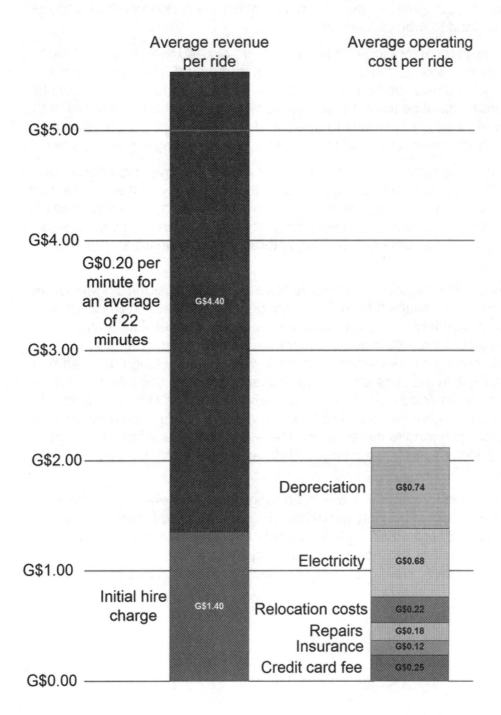

The average revenue per journey is G$5.80 and the average cost to Runnabout is G$2.19.

The software in Runnabout's hoverboards restricts the maximum speed of travel to 6 miles per hour (approximately 10 kilometres per hour). That is faster than a typical brisk walking pace of 3 to 4 miles per hour. The hoverboards could travel at much greater speeds, but Runnabout is concerned that a higher speed would lead to more accidents.

Runnabout requires users to be at least 18 years old and to have a valid car driver's licence. Although there is no legal requirement for users to be of a minimum age or to hold an official driving licence, Runnabout's insurers would charge more in the absence of those requirements. Runnabout is insured both against claims arising from injury to users and damage to their property and public liability insurance that covers injury or property damage to third parties.

The insurance cost stated above refers to the insurance cover provided to users with respect to any injury caused by the user to a third party or damage to third party property. This cover applies automatically for the duration of any valid hire by a user. Runnabout also incurs significant cost for insurance against claims made against the company by users or by third parties for injury or property damage.

To date, all of Runnabout's hoverboards have been purchased from Minnerring Robotics, a major manufacturer of industrial equipment based in Deeland, a country that is strongly associated with excellence in engineering. Minnerring has no connection with Runnabout, other than as a supplier. Runnabout selected Minnerring's hoverboard because it was a robust design that had been designed for use in factories as personal transportation for security staff and supervisors. When ridden carefully on flat surfaces such as tiled or concreted floors, Minnerring's hoverboards could be used for 40 hours a week for up to 6 months before they had to be replaced. The average depreciation charge of G$0.74 per ride is based on estimates of life expectancy provided by Minnerring.

Minnerring sells its hoverboards to a wide range of customers around the world, although Runnabout is the only customer who uses them to facilitate shared-hoverboard services. Minnerring hoverboards are used extensively in industrial and retail settings. For example, many security departments equip their officers with Minnerring hoverboards for patrol and fast-response duties.

Extracts from Runnabout's annual report

Runnabout's vision, mission and values

Vision

To keep Geeland moving.

Mission

Runnabout's mission is to offer an economical and efficient approach to micromobility. We wish to harness both new and existing technologies to enrich our users' lives while creating wealth for our shareholders.

Values

Runnabout will:

1.   provide users with safe and convenient transportation,

2.   minimise the environmental footprint of its micromobility solutions,

3.   protect the safety and dignity of its employees,

4.   engage with stakeholders to the mutual benefit of all.

Runnabout's Board of Directors

Jack Avery, Non-Executive Chairman

Jack is a retired business executive who was CEO of Capital City Buses, which operates an extensive network of buses across Greater Capital City.

During his period of leadership, Capital City Buses increased the number of buses in service by 22%.

Jack was appointed by Runnabout in 2017.

Mei Yee, Chief Executive Officer

Mei worked as a senior logistics manager in a courier company in Geeland for 16 years. She then joined Runnabout in 2018.

Geo Pataros, Chief Financial Officer

Geo was a senior accountant with an electric scooter manufacturer before he was appointed to Runnabout's Board. He is a qualified accountant.

Geo was appointed in 2019.

Alan Peters, Director of Operations

Alan is a traffic engineer by training. He worked for Western City Council for twenty years, working on a range of responsibilities including road planning and public transport management.

Alan joined Runnabout's Board in 2015.

Shaun McDougall, IT Director

Shaun has held a number of senior positions in major quoted companies including gaming companies. He enjoys a challenge and was delighted to join the Board in 2018.

Pat Olly, Human Resource Director

Pat has held senior HR roles in a number of organisations. She joined Runnabout as Human Resource Director in 2017.

Marco Palermo, Independent Non-Executive Director

Marco is a qualified accountant who was a partner in one of Geeland's leading accountancy firms before he retired from full-time employment.

Marco was appointed to Runnabout's Board in 2017.

Juliana Leung, Independent Non-Executive Director

Juliana founded a successful transport company. She retired in 2013 and was appointed to Runnabout's Board in 2016.

Patrick Chiu, Independent Non-Executive Director

Patrick was a senior manager in Geeland's Health Service, specialising in financial management. He was appointed to Runnabout's Board in 2017.

Organisation chart

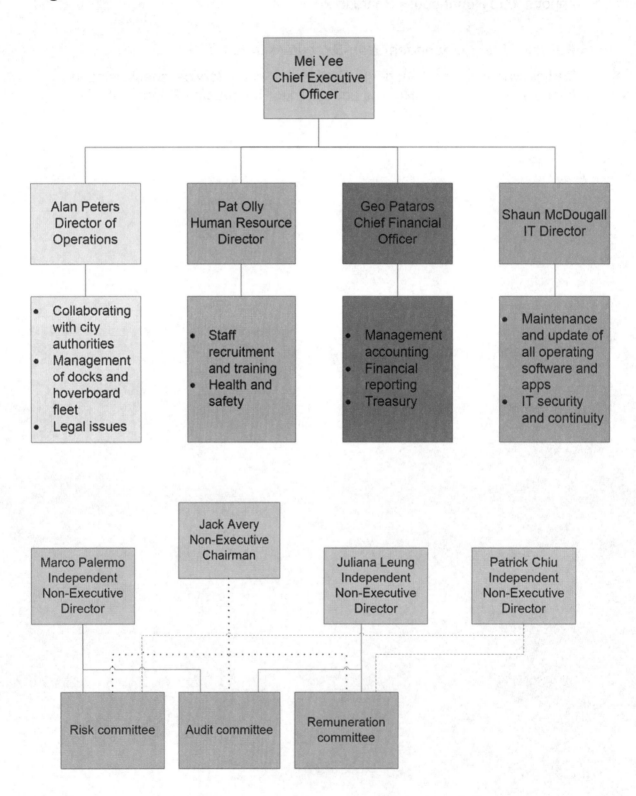

Runnabout's Principal Risks (extracted from annual report)

Risk theme	Risk impact	Risk mitigation
Safety	Hoverboards can cause injury and property damage when ridden irresponsibly.	Users must be at least 18 years old and hold a driver's licence before they can register as users.
	Hoverboards can injure pedestrians because they travel at relatively high speed on pavements and in pedestrianised areas.	Runnabout has comprehensive insurance cover for both injury and property damage.
	Hoverboards are powered by high capacity rechargeable batteries that can be prone to catching fire or exploding. They are particularly dangerous when dismantled or handled roughly.	All employees are fully trained in the safe handling of hoverboards. The hoverboards themselves have self-diagnostic sensors that can provide warning of problems with electrical connections and battery temperature.
Regulation and licensing	Runnabout requires the permission of city authorities in order to locate docks in convenient locations and offer the hire of vehicles for use on public pavements and pedestrianised areas. If that permission is withdrawn by any given city then operations would have to cease.	Runnabout maintains strong communication links with the local authorities. Runnabout's Board takes care to ensure that any concerns raised by the authorities are addressed as a matter of priority.
Competition	Runnabout has to compete with other providers of micromobility services, as well as traditional public transport, taxi and ride-sharing services. Competitors may take advantage of developments in technology and may receive subsidies from the government or city authorities.	Runnabout is the only provider of shared hoverboards in the cities in which it operates. That has a number of advantages. Hoverboards are the only vehicles that can be ridden on pavements, and so do not expose users to the risks of riding on the roads. They are also unaffected by delays caused by heavy traffic.

IT	Runnabout's operations are wholly dependent upon the availability of its servers and users' access to mobile phone networks in order to operate their apps.	The servers are backed up to a remote hot backup site that can take over in the event of the main site becoming unavailable. Mobile phone networks rarely go out of service. Those rare outages that do occur rarely affect more than one service provider, so it would be unlikely to prevent all users from hiring hoverboards.
	Runnabout's files contain sensitive data about users, including credit card details and the location of users when they hire and return hoverboards.	Runnabout ensures that its servers are secure. Staff are subject to background checks to ensure that they are trustworthy before they are granted access to users' data.

Runnabout's internal audit charter

Internal Audit is overseen by Runnabout's Audit Committee. The Chief Internal Auditor reports to Marco Palermo, the convener of the Audit Committee.

The Chief Internal Auditor is responsible for the management and organisation of internal audit staff. Internal Audit investigations will be conducted in accordance with appropriate professional audit standards.

The members of the Internal Audit Department are granted unrestricted access to any records, locations and assets that they deem necessary in order to discharge their duties. They are also free to interview all staff and have a right to receive full cooperation whenever they do so.

Audit staff will submit a written report to the Chief Internal Auditor at the conclusion of each audit investigation. The Chief Internal Auditor will provide the Convener of the Audit Committee with a summary of all audit reports, in addition to copying the full reports to the Convener.

Internal audit reports will be used to provide feedback to managers who are responsible for the areas subject to audit. Where exceptions are noted, the managers responsible will agree a plan for rectification and the internal audit staff will ensure that agreed changes are implemented.

An internal audit plan will be developed each year and approved by the Audit Committee. The plan will focus on areas identified using a risk-based approach. The Chief Internal Auditor will seek authorisation from the Convener of the Audit Committee before deviating from the plan. The Audit Committee has the authority to require revisions to the plan or to request special investigations that are deemed necessary.

Financial statements

The following information has been extracted from Runnabout Group's financial statements for the year ended 31 December 2019

Runnabout Group
Consolidated statement of profit or loss
for the year ended 31 December

	2019 G$ million	2018 G$ million
Revenue	97,943	85,211
Cost of goods sold	(39,908)	(34,323)
Marketing expenses	(5,083)	(4,175)
Administration expenses	(21,055)	(20,213)
Operating profit	31,897	26,500
Financial expense	(5,623)	(2,892)
Profit before tax	26,274	23,608
Tax	(6,831)	(6,883)
Profit for the year	19,443	16,725

Runnabout Group
Consolidated statement of changes in equity
for the year ended 31 December 2019

	Share capital G$ million	Retained earnings G$ million	Total G$ million
Opening balance	10,000	29,143	39,143
Profit for year		19,443	19,443
Dividend		(7,095)	(7,095)
Closing balance	10,000	41,491	51,491

Runnabout Group
Consolidated statement of financial position
as at 31 December

	2019 G$ million	2018 G$ million
Non-current assets		
Property, plant and equipment	128,790	109,471
Intangible assets	1,621	1,508
	130,411	110,979
Current assets		
Inventories	389	306
Trade receivables	9,821	9,035
Cash and cash equivalents	2,325	2,622
	12,535	11,963
Total assets	142,946	122,942
Equity		
Share capital	10,000	10,000
Retained earnings	41,491	29,143
	51,491	39,143
Non-current liabilities		
Loans	62,475	55,475
Deferred tax	15,079	15,012
	77,554	70,487
Current liabilities		
Trade payables	7,056	6,421
Current tax	6,845	6,891
	13,901	13,312
Total equity and liabilities	142,946	122,942

Major competitor

Runnabout is the only provider of hoverboard-sharing services in Geeland, but it is not the only provider of micromobility services. Dokbyke operates an electric bicycle-sharing scheme in Capital City and five other major cities.

Dokbyke Group
Consolidated statement of profit or loss
for the year ended 31 December

	2019	2018
	G$ million	G$ million
Revenue	28,403	23,859
Cost of goods sold	(9,788)	(7,624)
Marketing expenses	(2,129)	(2,019)
Administration expenses	(5,913)	(5,475)
Operating profit	10,573	8,741
Financial expense	(1,079)	(1,298)
Profit before tax	9,494	7,443
Tax	(2,468)	(1,935)
Profit for the year	7,026	5,508

Dokbyke Group
Consolidated statement of financial position
as at 31 December

	2019 G$ million	2018 G$ million
Non-current assets		
Property, plant and equipment	24,470	24,084
Intangible assets	1,426	1,312
	25,896	25,396
Current assets		
Inventories	86	74
Trade receivables	3,143	3,072
Cash and cash equivalents	419	420
	3,648	3,566
Total assets	29,544	28,962
Equity		
Share capital	800	800
Retained earnings	7,860	5,229
	8,660	6,029
Non-current liabilities		
Loans	11,993	14,424
Deferred tax	4,222	4,504
	16,215	18,928
Current liabilities		
Trade payables	2,187	2,058
Current tax	2,482	1,947
	4,669	4,005
Total equity and liabilities	29,544	28,962

Share price history

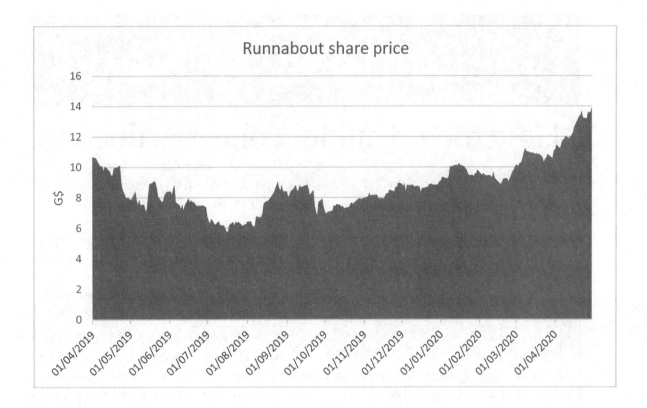

Runnabout's geared beta is 1.33. Its ungeared beta is 1.21.

News stories

Geeland Daily News

'Hoverboard ankle' concerns doctors

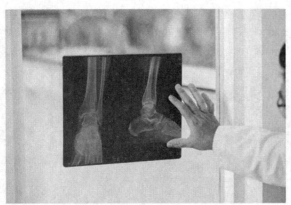

Hospital emergency rooms have reported a steady increase in the number of ankle injuries caused by hoverboard users crossing roads by jumping off the kerb at maximum speed. This affects children playing with toy hoverboards near their homes and adults using larger hoverboards in city centres.

When hoverboards are ridden like this over time the springs that absorb the impact of jumping from the pavement down to the road weaken and sometimes even break. That puts users at risk of injury because the impact is then absorbed by their ankles, leading to sprains and broken bones.

Doctors blame the increase in injuries on the fact that users are becoming more confident in their riding ability and are taking greater risks.

Runnabout, the shared-hoverboard provider, advises its users that hoverboards should never be ridden over obstacles such as kerbs. If users need to cross the road they should either do so using a pedestrian crossing that has a lowered kerb or wait until the road is clear and carry their hoverboard to the opposite side.

IT Monthly

Dokbyke CIO criticises lack of qualified graduates

Titus Mohubedu, Chief Information Officer at Dokbyke, Geeland's largest bicycle-sharing service, spoke out against the many "irrelevant" degree courses in IT that are offered by some universities. In his opinion, many IT degrees are far too theoretical and pay insufficient attention to the real-world issues that matter to IT managers. He was speaking at the launch of the collaborative degree course that Dokbyke was sponsoring at the University of Capital City. This combines academic study with structured practical experience at Dokbyke's data centres. It is hoped that the course will attract 150 students each year, most of whom will work for Dokbyke when they graduate.

Mr Mohubedu pointed out that many service providers, including Dokbyke and similar entities, were wholly dependent upon the efficiency of their IT infrastructure. He said that Dokbyke employed more staff in IT than it did in maintaining and servicing its bicycles. Dokbyke's IT spend amounts to 14% of its total operating costs.

Geeland Telegraph

Business News

Banks criticise credit card customers

A recent report by the banking industry has demonstrated that many credit card customers took a very careless view of the security features that are built into their cards. The two largest issuers have more than 500 million cardholders between them, so that could represent a significant exposure to fraudulent transactions.

Typical cardholder errors include:

- Physical security – many cardholders leave their wallets and purses in plain sight in their homes, which means that burglars can steal their credit cards, along with the other data that can be used to validate a telephone payment, such as their dates of birth and postal addresses.

- Failing to sign the signature strip on the back of their card – those signatures are rarely examined, but they are there to help confirm the cardholder's identity and there is no need to make life easy for a thief.

- Carelessness with the 3-digit security number on the back of the card – contrary to popular belief, the 16 digit number on the front of the card is rarely sufficient on its own to validate an online or telephone payment, but having the extra three digits is often sufficient to validate a payment.

- Writing down the PIN number – it is commonplace for cardholders to carry a piece of paper with their personal identification number (PIN) in their wallet or to have their PIN written in their diary.

The banks have warned that their losses from credit card fraud are unsustainable and that cardholders who are careless may be held liable for some or all of any unauthorised charges made against their accounts.

Geeland Telegraph

Bicycles make city streets safer for all

A research study published by the University of Western City suggests that micromobility was changing the nature of accidents involving pedestrians. There is a strong negative correlation between the numbers of bicycles and the number of pedestrians being knocked down by motor vehicles. That has been attributed to the "traffic calming" effects of motorists driving more slowly because of the difficulties of overtaking groups of cyclists safely. There have been fewer cases of pedestrians being knocked down by motor vehicles while crossing the road.

Unfortunately, the pavements themselves are becoming increasingly dangerous because of hoverboards. The danger is that pedestrians who step to the side to let hoverboards pass are at risk of stepping into the paths of bicycles that are approaching silently from behind.

Overall, there is no evidence that city streets are becoming more dangerous, but all road and pavement users are reporting an increase in the perceived risk of travelling at busy times.

Geeland Telegraph

City Councillor clashes with Transport Minister

A row has broken out between Geeland's Transport Minister and the Councillor who is responsible for oversight of the Capital City Street Safety (CCSS) department at Capital City Council. The dispute is over the need for regulation of the siting of docks to support micromobility schemes on city streets.

The Transport Minister, who is responsible for governing transportation at a national level, wishes to impose more stringent rules relating to the maximum size of docks and the minimum distance from roads. The City Councillor objects on the grounds that city councils should retain the power to decide such matters, taking account of the needs of local pedestrians and local traffic conditions.

This debate is unlikely to be resolved soon. There are important democratic principles at stake, which are not helped by the fact that the ruling party in charge of Capital City Council is not the same as the party in charge of Geeland's national parliament.

Extracts from Whiny Turner's Blog

Personal best!

I had my fastest run yet from the railway station to my office. I hired a trusty Runnabout hoverboard as usual and, by luck, the pavements were quieter than usual. It only took me 18 minutes to get to the dock outside the office instead of the usual 20 minutes or more. Admittedly, the hoverboard felt pretty hot when I redocked it. That must be why the machine was making that beeping noise when I was pushing it hard up the slight incline to the junction with Harper Street!

COMMENTS

I think the beeping noise means that the battery is overheating. I don't think that Runnabout can complain if we push their machines hard because we pay by the minute. Shaving two minutes off your run would save you a fair amount over a week.

Street Surfer

Whiny, we should race one day!

Rubber Burner

Warm jumper

I had my first serious "incident" today, trying to get back to the station in time to catch the early train. I had to cross Pike Street and was heading for the pedestrian crossing when the road cleared. Rather than risk getting caught at the lights, I turned and jumped the hoverboard I was riding from the pavement down to the road. I have made that manoeuvre many times, but the pavement was higher than I had expected and I hit the road with a crash. I managed to stay upright, but the hoverboard's platform was badly broken and it would have been crazy to have tried to ride it like that. I ended up carrying the hoverboard to the nearest dock and returning it. The battery was really hot, although I wasn't riding all that hard.

Needless to say, I missed my train.

COMMENTS

You might get a letter from Runnabout. They will know that you were the last person to ride that hoverboard, unless somebody else is stupid enough to take it out in that condition. My advice is to say that it was like that when you hired it.

Sad Eric

I think that you were lucky. The hoverboard probably had a short circuit after the crash and that made it overheat. You could have been burned.

Throttle Master

Putting on weight?

 I left for the station at the same time as a colleague today. We like to race to the station and it is usually a good contest because there is rarely more than a few seconds between us. Tonight, my colleague forgot that he was wearing a rucksack full of books that he had collected for charity. It must have weighed at least 30 kg.

Anyway, he couldn't understand why he was unable to keep up with me. When I told him that Runnabout has a 95 kg weight limit, which is highlighted during Runnabout's initial registration process, he said that he weighs only 80 kg. He couldn't understand that he had to count the weight of his rucksack too.

COMMENTS

Runnabout says that the maximum weight is 95 kg, but it is probably ok to exceed that by 5 kg or so. Your colleague almost certainly overloaded the hoverboard to breaking point. He was lucky not to have lost a wheel or broken the platform because falling off a hoverboard while travelling at 6 miles per hour will always be unpleasant.

Boy Racer

May and August 2020 real exam – analysing the pre-seen

Chapter learning objectives

- to understand various techniques and models that can help familiarisation with the pre-seen.

1   The importance of familiarisation

The pre-seen material is released approximately seven weeks before you sit the exam and one of your first tasks will be to analyse the context within which the case is set. Although your responses in the exam will be driven by the unseen material, you will only be able to fully assess the impact of each event on the organisation if you have a sufficient depth of knowledge and awareness of both the organisation and the industry in which it operates.

The purpose of the pre-seen material is to allow you to gain that knowledge and awareness. Remember, you will be acting in the position of a senior finance manager who advises the highest level of management. It will therefore be expected that you will have some familiarity with the industry and business.

It is extremely important that you study the pre-seen material thoroughly before you go into the examination. There are two main reasons for this:

- It will save time in the examination itself if you are already familiar with the pre-seen material (there will be approximately 25-30 pages of information in the pre-seen, so a lot of information to absorb).

- It enables you to develop a view of the situation facing the organisation in the case study.

You will not be able to respond to the examination tasks from the pre-seen material alone; the unseen material given to you in the examination will present significant new information that may alter the situation substantially. Even so, a major step towards success in the examination is a careful study, exploration and understanding of the pre-seen material.

Each set of pre-seen material is different but as a general rule, you can expect the following:

- Industry background

- History of the business

- Key personnel

- Organisational structure

- Key risks facing the business

- Financial Statements

- Press articles addressing issues facing the industry

Each of these areas will need reviewing in detail.

You should question what each piece of information tells you, and why the examiner may have given it to you.

2 Exhibit by exhibit analysis

The purpose of this initial stage is to lay a foundation for further analysis. It's more about asking questions than finding solutions. Before you do anything else, you should read the pre-seen material from beginning to end without making any notes, simply to familiarise yourself with the scenario.

Read the material again, as many times as you think necessary, without making notes. You can do this over a period of several days, if you wish.

When you think you are reasonably familiar with the situation described by the material, you should start to make notes. By making notes, you will become more familiar with the detail of the scenario.

- Try to make notes on each paragraph (or each group of short paragraphs) in the pre-seen material.

- Ask yourself "why might the examiner have told me this?"

- Try to make your questions as broad as possible; consider as many different stakeholders as possible and try to put yourself in different positions (say the CEO, a customer, an employee, etc.) to consider the information from different perspectives.

Illustration 1 – Runnabout: Introductory overview

Given below is an example of some questions you could ask yourself relating to the second and third exhibits of the question tutorial exam pre-seen information.

Question	Potential response
What sector of industry does Runnabout operate in?	It operates in the micromobility sector, which involves travellers renting some sort of device (such as a bicycle or scooter) to complete their journey (p41)
Is Runnabout a well-established company?	It was established in 2005 and was listed on the Geeland Stock Exchange in 2010 (p46).
Which particular sector of the micromobility market does it operate in?	It began with bicycles in 2005, then began moving into hoverboards in 2016. (p.46&47).
How many cities does Runnabout operate in?	15 cities, all in Geeland (p.47)
Who can operate a Runnabout hoverboard?	Anyone who is 18 or over and has a valid car driver's licence (p.50)

3 Note taking

When you're making notes, try to be as creative as possible. Psychologists tell us that using conventional linear notes on their own use only a small part of our mental capacity. They are hard to remember and prevent us from drawing connections between topics. This is because they seek to classify things under hierarchical headings.

Here are some techniques that candidates find useful. See which ones work for you as you practise on the question tutorial case in this text.

Spider diagrams

Spider diagrams (or clustering diagrams) are a quick graphic way of summarising connections between subjects. You cannot put much detail into a spider diagram, just a few key words. However, it does help you to 'visualise' the information in the case material. You must expect to update your spider diagram as you go along and to redraft it when it starts to get too messy. It is all part of the learning process.

Timelines

Timelines are valuable to make sense of the sequence of events in the pre-seen and to understand where the company in the case study presently stands. The case study exam takes place in real time, so you need to be clear how long is likely to elapse between the data in the pre-seen and the actual exam. This is the time period during which the issues facing the company can be incorporated into the unseen material.

Colours

Colours help you remember things you may want to draw upon in the exam room. You could write down all your financial calculations and observations in green whilst having red for organisational and blue for strategic. Some candidates use different colour highlighter pens to emphasise different aspects of the pre-seen material perhaps using the same colour coding suggestion.

Additionally, sometimes making notes in different colours helps you to remember key facts and some of the preparation that you have done using the pre-seen material.

Use whatever colours work for you – but it does help to make notes on both the pre-seen material and the research you do. DO NOT just read the material – you must take notes (in whatever format) and if colours help you to understand and link your research together then use colours.

4   Technical analysis

Now you're reasonably familiar with the material it's time to carry out some technical analysis to help you identify and understand the issues facing the company.

A good starting point is to revise any 'technical' topics that might be relevant. The pre-seen material might imply that a particular 'technical' issue could be relevant in the exam, such as commenting on the corporate governance of a company, financing, hedging, business valuations, and so on. Anticipate exam tasks by asking yourself how you would apply your knowledge in such areas in the context of the live case.

If you lack confidence on any topic that might be relevant, go back to your previous study materials and revise it if necessary.

Exercise 1 – Runnabout: technical topic analysis
Typical technical topic areas could include the following.
1   Discuss the financing structure at Runnabout and Dokbyke (F3).
2   Discuss the level of dividend payout at Runnabout (F3).
3   Evaluate the corporate governance structure at Runnabout (P3).
4   Discuss Runnabout's exposure to risk and suitable mitigations (other than the risks included in the Principal Risks extract in the annual report (P3).
5   Identify possible strategies for growth for Runnabout (E3).

5   Financial analysis

You will almost certainly be given some figures in the pre-seen material. These might relate to the company's profits or losses, or product profitability. There might be statements of profit or loss and statements of financial position for previous years, statements of changes in equity, cash flow statements, share price graphs, and so on. You might also be given similar information for a competitor.

A key part of your initial analysis will be to perform some simple financial analysis, such as financial ratio calculations or a cash flow analysis. These might give you a picture of changes in profitability, liquidity, working capital management or cash flows over time, and will help ensure you have a rounded picture of the organisation's current position.

If a cash flow statement is not provided, it may be worth preparing a summary of cash flows. You may have to make some assumptions if the detailed information isn't provided but even with these, there is great value in appreciating where the money has come from, and where it is being spent.

Profitability ratios

You might find useful information from an analysis of profit/sales ratios, for:

- the company as a whole

- each division, or

- each product or service.

Profit margins can be measured as a net profit percentage and as a gross profit percentage. ROCE is also a fundamental profitability ratio to be considered. You can then look at trends in the ratios over time, or consider whether the margins are good or disappointing.

Analysing the ratio of certain expenses to sales might also be useful, such as the ratio of administration costs to sales, sales and marketing costs to sales or R&D costs to sales. Have there been any noticeable changes in these ratios over time and, if so, is it clear why the changes have happened?

Working capital ratios

Working capital ratios can be calculated to assess the efficiency of working capital management (= management of inventory, trade receivables and trade payables). They can also be useful for assessing liquidity, because excessive investment in working capital ties up cash and slows the receipt of cash.

The main working capital ratios are:

- "inventory days" or the average inventory holding period: a long period might indicate poor inventory management

- "receivable days" or the average time that customers take to pay: a long period could indicate issues with the collection of cash, although would need to consider this in light of the entity's credit terms and industry averages

- "payable days" or the average time to pay suppliers: a long period could indicate cash flow difficulties for the entity, although would need to consider in light of credit terms.

You should be familiar with these ratios and how to calculate the length of the cash cycle or operating cycle.

Cash flow analysis or funding analysis

If the main objective of a company is to maximise the wealth of its shareholders, the most important financial issues will be profitability and returns to shareholders. However, other significant issues in financial strategy are often:

- cash flows and liquidity, and

- gearing

A possible cash flow problem occurs whenever the cash flows from operations do not appear to be sufficient to cover all the non-operational cash payments that the company has to make, such as spending on capital expenditure items.

An analysis of future funding can be carried out by looking at the history of changes in the statement of financial position.

Ratio analysis – a warning!

Candidates are advised to resist typing out ratios in the exam unless they are actually relevant to the task. It's always impressive when a candidate uses a ratio to reinforce a point, but it's a waste of time to produce a couple of ratios just because you can!

Exercise 2 – Runnabout: Ratio Analysis

Use ratio analysis to assess the profit performance of Runnabout for 2019 and 2018, and compare it to that of Dokbyke. Write a brief commentary on your findings.

6   Industry analysis and research

Why is industry research important?

Remember, part of your preparatory work is to analyse the context within which the case is set. A full analysis is not possible without an understanding of the industry and research may support the information provided in the pre-seen. From this analysis, you may be better able to understand the key issues and address the requirements.

The pre-seen material usually contains a good summary of relevant information about the industry. This can be relied on as accurate at the time it is published and will form the basis of your analysis. At the strategic level the scope of this industry information will be fairly extensive, as the industry data provided with the pre-seen will be more detailed and varied to support analysis of the business from a strategic perspective.

You could further research the industry setting for the case you are working on so that you can develop a better understanding of the problems (and opportunities) facing companies in this industry. Hopefully, it will also stop you from making unrealistic comments in your answer on the day of the exam.

Industry research will allow you to add further comments in terms of:

- identifying potential problems currently facing the industry

- identifying the nature of competition and the basis for customer and supplier relationships

- considering the competitive strategies being followed by companies operating in the real world and how they are achieved (e.g. special technologies, use of brands) and whether they could be adopted by the company in the pre-seen

- identifying issues with operational aspects of real world firms.

How to conduct industry research

Your research could incorporate any of the following sources of information:

- *Personal networks / experience*

  If you happen to work in the industry described, then you could talk to colleagues about the case. If not, then perhaps family or friends with relevant experience could help.

  Alternatively, it may be that you have been a customer in the industry described. For Runnabout, many students would have had experience of hiring a pay-as-you-go bicycle and so would appreciate some of the issues involved.

- *Using the Internet*

  This is the most convenient and commonly used method of researching the industry, but as noted above, try to target the information you're looking for in order to avoid wasting time. Generally, you will be looking for the following sorts of information:

  - Websites of firms similar to the one(s) in the pre-seen material. This can help you learn about the sorts of products and competitive strategies they follow and may also yield financial information that can be compared with the data in the pre-seen material.

  - Trade journals of the industry in the pre-seen. This will provide information on real world environmental issues facing the business.

  - Articles on the industry in journals and newspapers. These will keep you up to date on developments.

  - Financial statements of real firms, perhaps even calculating key ratios.

Illustration 2 – Runnabout: Real world websites

Relevant websites for the micromobility industry include the following:

The Industry – hoverboard manufacturers

https://www.hoverboards.co.uk/about-us

https://www.razor.com/products/hoverboards/

http://uk-en.segway.com/

https://www.epikgo.com/

https://swagtron.com/product-category/hoverboard/

https://gotrax.com/collections/hoverboards

The Industry – mobility sharing

http://iskooter.com/ – hoverboard sharing in Las Vegas

https://mobike.com/uk/

https://www.jump.com/gb/en/

https://www.bird.co/

https://www.li.me/en-us/home

https://www.spin.app/

Newspaper articles

https://www.theguardian.com/uk-news/2015/oct/12/uk-hoverboard-crackdown-all-you-need-to-know

https://www.theguardian.com/technology/2016/jan/14/hoverboard-explodes-into-flames-on-first-run

https://www.theguardian.com/us-news/2020/jan/08/electric-scooter-injuries-soar-study

https://www.theguardian.com/world/2019/jun/06/paris-taking-steps-to-crack-down-on-electric-scooter-providers

https://www.thetimes.co.uk/article/boy-15-on-hoverboard-dies-in-bus-collision-mw3mkshsg7v

https://www.telegraph.co.uk/technology/2019/07/14/ban-privately-owned-cars-city-centres-says-uber-executive/

https://www.theguardian.com/uk-news/2018/nov/27/electric-bike-sharing-company-lime-launch-uk

https://www.theguardian.com/world/2020/feb/02/e-scooters-fears-pubic-safety-crisis-road-approval-uk

YouTube

https://www.youtube.com/watch?v=Ae0f9NMn6Kl **– some sound buying advice for consumers**

https://www.youtube.com/watch?v=_LfTtej5Q0I

https://www.youtube.com/watch?v=6BxWvxzcFgM

Other websites

https://www.bbc.co.uk/news/uk-47624566

https://www2.deloitte.com/us/en/insights/focus/future-of-mobility/micro-mobility-is-the-future-of-urban-transportation.html **– an interesting article on micromobility in general**

https://www.mckinsey.com/industries/automotive-and-assembly/our-insights/micromobilitys-15000-mile-checkup **– an article by McKinsey & Co. on micromobility in general**

http://ridenfly.co.uk/ **– a business that organises hoverboard riding events**

7 Ethical analysis

Ethical issues could relate to any of the following areas:

- corporate social responsibility;
- personal ethical behaviour of individuals in the case;
- business ethics.

Before the exam, you should take some time to remind yourself of CIMA's Guidelines on ethical conduct. You can download a copy of the Ethical Guidelines from CIMA's website, if you want to read the full text. Although these are useful, you must remember that the ethical issues in the exam are not necessarily ethical issues facing the management accountant, but more issues facing the business as a whole. An awareness of general 'corporate ethics' and 'corporate and social responsibility' will therefore be beneficial.

Illustration 3 – Runnabout: Real world ethical issues

Online research into hoverboards quickly reveals ethical (and legal) issues related to the safety of the product, both for its users and people close by. For example:

https://www.theguardian.com/technology/2016/jan/14/hoverboard-explodes-into-flames-on-first-run

8   Position audit

Once you've analysed all of the above you're ready to carry out a position audit.

CIMA defines a position audit as:

Part of the planning process which examines the current state of the entity in respect of:

- resources of tangible and intangible assets and finance,

- products brands and markets,

- operating systems such as production and distribution,

- internal organisation,

- current results,

- returns to shareholders.

What you should be attempting to do is stand back so you can appreciate the bigger picture of the organisation. You can do this by considering four main headings – Strengths, Weaknesses, Opportunities and Threats. This is usually referred to as a SWOT analysis. Within your SWOT analysis you should look for:

- Threat homing in upon weakness – the potential for failure.

- Threat on a strength – should be able to defend against it but remember competencies slip.

- Opportunity on a strength – areas they should be able to exploit.

- Opportunity on a weakness – areas where they could exploit in the future if they can change.

In addition to preparing a SWOT analysis, it is useful to prepare a two-three page summary of your analysis. Try not to simply repeat information from the pre-seen but add value by including your thoughts on the analysis you've performed.

Exercise 3 – Runnabout: SWOT analysis
Perform a SWOT analysis for Runnabout.

9 Main issues and précis

Once you've prepared your summary you are finally able to consider the key issues facing the organisation. Your conclusion on the main issues arising from the pre-seen will direct your focus and aid your understanding of issues in the exam.

Once you've got a list of the main issues, give yourself more time to think. Spend some time thinking about the case study, as much as you can. You don't have to be sitting at a desk or table to do this. You can think about the case study when you travel to work or in any spare time that you have for thinking.

- When new ideas come to you, jot them down.

- If you think of a new approach to financial analysis, carry out any calculations you think might be useful.

Remember, all of the above preparatory work enables you to feel as if you really are a management accountant working for this organisation. Without the prep, you're unlikely to be convincing in this role. However, please note that there is a danger that research can encourage time wasting in the exam itself. There is no point in providing irrelevant facts in an answer just because you have worked on them as part of your preparation!

Illustration 4 – Runnabout: Summary

The industry

Micromobility is a relatively recent phenomenon, and is used for short journeys that supplement the last part of a bigger one. For example, commuters might travel by train or bus to a station or bus stop, then use an alternative form of transport to take them to their precise destination.

The sector was first created with the introduction of bike sharing services. A user could collect a bike from a strategically-located docking station, then drop it off at another docking station, close to their destination. This provided an alternative to using local buses, taxis etc., and was considered a preferable and environmentally friendly way to travel the last mile.

In the UK, the most notable example was the introduction of the so-called 'Boris Bikes' in London. This has now been replicated in many other towns and cities.

Other forms of micromobility entered the sector, such as electric bikes and electric scooters. This meant that docking stations had to be adapted so as to allow for recharging of the machines.

Customers pay for the amount of time that a machine is on hire, so it is a flexible and possibly cheaper alternative to owning their own machine.

A principal benefit to society is that it cuts down on congestion and pollution, although the issue of safety to pedestrians and riders has not been fully resolved.

The company

Runnabout was formed in 2005, and started life as a bike sharing company using conventional bicycles. It floated on the Geeland Stock Exchange in 2010, at which point it had a presence in 15 cities in Geeland.

In 2012 it introduced a number of electric bikes, and so had to adapt its docking stations to be able to accommodate these. The government of Geeland then introduced legislation that made it compulsory for cyclists to wear helmets, which lead to a fall in demand. At the same time, competitors started to emerge in Geeland.

To combat this, the company changed from offering bike sharing services to hoverboard sharing. It no longer offers bike sharing at all.

A hoverboard is a two-wheeled machine with a platform that the rider stands on. Control over speed and direction is via balance – lean forward to go forwards, lean left to turn left, etc. Not only have they proved popular with typical travellers who need to get to work; they have also been popular with tourists and shoppers.

Runnabout is still present in the same 15 cities as in 2010.

The business model

Users of Runnabout services need to register with the company, which they can do so via an app on their mobile phone. Personal details are collected, including debit/credit card information.

When a user wishes to hire a hoverboard, they input a 4-digit location code for the relevant docking station into the app. After verifying the user's identity, the company's server sends a 5-digit one-time code to the user's phone, which releases a hoverboard and starts the period of hire.

The hire period ends when the user places the hoverboard into a docking station, and charges are then automatically made against the retained card details.

Runnabout has over 30 million registered users. Users have to be at least 18 years old and have a valid car driver's licence to be approved.

Runnabout is insured against damage and injury to users and third parties for valid hires.

The company sources all of its hoverboards from Minnerring Robotics, a company based in Deeland. Minnerring was chosen because of its products' robust design.

Financial performance

Runnabout reported revenues of $98 billion in 2019, which represented growth of 14% over the previous year. Operating profit grew by 20% over the same period. Interest cover fell from 9.2 times to 5.7 times as further long term debt finance was taken out.

The dividend for the year just gone was just over $7 billion, representing a pay-out ratio of 36.5% of profit for the year.

The company has $2.3 bn of cash in the bank, and a financial gearing ratio (measured as debt ÷ debt + equity) of 55%.

Overall, the performance and position of the company look healthy, although it is questionable whether further debt finance should be raised at the current levels of gearing.

A graph is given of the company's share price performance over the last year. The share price has doubled in the last 6 months, from around $7/share to $14/share. Beta information is given about the company; its geared beat is 1.33, and its ungeared beta 1.21.

Competition

Financial statements are given in respect of a competitor, Dokbyke. However, Dokbyke is not a direct competitor, as Runnabout has a monopoly over hoverboard sharing services in Geeland. Dokbyke offers bike sharing services, and has enjoyed stronger growth in both revenues and profits than Runnabout. However, it is only present in 6 Geeland cities, and so may be at an earlier stage in the business life cycle than Runnabout.

Other issues

A recurrent theme throughout the case is political risk. Each city's local authority grants a licence to micromobility companies to operate; at present, each of the 15 authorities where Runnabout is present is refusing to grant a licence to other hoverboard sharing businesses. So Runnabout has the market to itself.

However, another theme is safety to the public. If authorities decide that having hoverboards on pavements is dangerous to members of the public, licences could be withdrawn quickly.

Another key theme is the safety of the product. Users have been injured through not riding boards properly, or using them for too long/too aggressively, resulting in the product overheating and bursting into flames.

10   Summary

You should now understand what you need to do in order to familiarise yourself with the pre-seen sufficiently.

Test your understanding answers

Exercise 1 – Runnabout: technical topic analysis

1   Discuss the financial gearing structure at Runnabout and Dokbyke.

Workings – Runnabout

All in G$m		2019		2018	
Gearing	D / E	62,475 / 51,491	121.3%	55,475 / 39,143	141.7%
(book values)	D / (D+E)	62,475 / (62,475 + 51,491)	54.8%	55,475 / (55,475 + 39,143)	58.6%
Interest cover	Operating profit / Finance cost	31,897 / 5,623	5.7 times	26,500 / 2,892	9.2 times
Interest rate (approx.)	(Finance cost / Year end loans balance) × 100%	(5,623 / 62,475) × 100%	9.0%	(2,892 / 55,475) × 100%	5.2%
Dividend cover	Profit for the year / Dividend	19,443 / 7,095	2.7 times		No information
Ungeared beta			1.21		No information
Geared beta			1.33		No information

Workings – Dokbyke

All in G$m		2019		2018	
Gearing	D / E	11,993 / 8,660	138.5%	14,424 / 6,029	239.2%
(book values)	D / (D+E)	11,993 / (11,993 + 8,660)	58.1%	14,424 / (14,424 + 6,029)	70.5%

Interest cover	Operating profit / Finance cost	10,573 / 1,079	9.8 times	8,741 / 1,298	6.7 times
Interest rate (approx.)	(Finance cost / Year end loans balance) × 100%	(1,079 / 11,993) × 100%	9.0%	(1,298 / 14,424) × 100%	9.0%
Dividend cover	Profit for the year / Dividend	7,026 / 4,395	1.6 times		No information
Ungeared beta			No information		No information
Geared beta			No information		No information

Commentary on long term funding

Debt finance

Gearing (statement of financial position)

Runnabout increased its debt finance between 2018 and 2019, but its gearing ratio has fallen because the book value of equity has also increased.

It would be preferable to measure gearing using market values, but without knowing the number of shares in issue, that doesn't seem possible here at first glance (but see later notes for an attempt to calculate the market value of equity of Runnabout).

Interest cover and interest rates

Runnabout's interest cover has fallen year on year despite the increase in operating profit. The reason for this is that the finance cost has almost doubled (from G$ 2,892 million to G$ 5,623 million). The estimated rate of interest paid by Runnabout in 2019 was 9.0% – well above the estimated 5.2% paid in 2018.

An increase in interest rate is sometimes an indicator that lenders perceive the company as more risky. However, in this case, Runnabout's share price has risen during 2019 and most of its other performance measures show an improving picture too. Dokbyke's interest rate is 9.0% too, so perhaps 9.0% is the general market rate of interest.

Equity finance

Dividend pay-outs

Share price

Runnabout is a listed company – a graph of its share price is shown on page 20 of the pre-seen.

The share price is currently approximately G\$ 14, which is the highest it has been at any point during the last year. Seemingly, the Runnabout shareholders are happy with the performance and prospects of the company.

Value of equity

It was noted above that we are not told how many shares Runnabout has, so we had to measure gearing on a book value basis rather than the more useful measure based on market values. However, using the information from page 20 of the pre-seen (share price graph and beta factors) we can estimate the market value of Runnabout's equity as shown below:

Workings:

From the F3 formula sheet we know that ungeared beta and geared beta are linked by the following formula:

$$\beta_{ungeared} = \left[\frac{V_E}{V_E + V_D[1 - T]} \right] \beta_{geared} + \left[\frac{V_D[1 - T]}{V_E + V_D[1 - T]} \right] \beta_d$$

If we make a few (sensible) assumptions, we can use this formula to estimate the market value of equity:

- On page 20 of the pre-seen we are told that Runnabout's geared beta is 1.33 and its ungeared beta is 1.21.

- We also know that Runnabout paid tax at a rate of 26.0% in 2019, so let's assume that $T = 0.26$.

- The risk associated with debt finance, especially in a well-established profitable listed company, is likely to be very small, so we can confidently assume that the debt beta is negligible (assume it is zero).

- Runnabout's borrowings are stated in the statement of financial position as G\$ 62,475 million. If these are bank borrowings, the market value will also be G\$ 62,475 million. If the borrowings are bonds, traded on the market, the market value might be different from book value (depending on market forces), but in the absence of any more information about the debt finance, let's assume that the market value is G\$ 62,475 million to enable us to calculate the value of equity.

Plugging all these numbers into the formula gives:

$$1.21 = \left[\frac{V_E}{V_E + 62,475m[1 - 0.26]}\right] 1.33$$

So

V_E = G$ 466,168 million

So if we measure gearing using market values rather than book values (debt to (debt plus equity)), it is 11.8% (62,475 / (62,475 + 466,168)) which is a very low level of gearing.

2   Discuss the level of dividend pay-out at Runnabout.

Introduction

Reduced to basics, the dividend decision is a balancing act. Given a certain amount of available profit, the question is how much should be paid to the shareholders and how much is needed to finance the future growth of the company? On the face of it, more dividends means less available for future investment and therefore lower levels of future growth (and therefore less profit available to pay future dividends).

However, this is further complicated by the availability of other sources of funds. If, for example, debt funds could be used to finance the future growth then less of the profit is needed so more can be paid as dividend.

The theory

There is no real theoretical answer to this balancing problem. The available theory (Modigliani & Miller's dividend irrelevance theory) claims that it's not a problem; if the company has available investment opportunities with positive NPVs then these should take precedence over dividends. However, the theory depends on a number of assumptions (the key ones being no differential taxes and no transaction cost) which are simply not valid in practice.

Thus the theory is of little practical use.

Possible choices

There are a number of different policies that could be followed. The main choice is between:

- Residual dividend:

  Here any available profits are first used to invest in positive NPV projects. A dividend is only paid if there are profits left after all available positive NPV projects have been undertaken.

  (This is following the theory mentioned above.)

- Constant pay-out ratio:

  Each year the dividend paid is a fixed proportion of that year's available profit.

- Stable dividends:

    The company pays a constant dividend each year, or a dividend growing at a constant rate.

The first two of these end up with varying and largely unpredictable dividends and if there is one thing the markets hate it is uncertainty (or risk). A stable dividend policy enables investors to predict with reasonable certainty what the return will be each year.

The practicality

In reality there are two main considerations:

- The clientele effect:

    This is the idea that, over time, a company with a given dividend policy (whatever that may be) will attract as its shareholders those investors who want that particular policy. Thus whatever policy the company chooses it should stick to it.

- The signalling effect:

    The shareholders think that the dividend declared each year reflects the directors' confidence in the future performance of the company. Thus dividends should not be varied year on year just because of short term fluctuations in company performance.

Both these considerations again reflect what was said above; stability is what investors want.

Runnabout's situation

Runnabout paid out G$ 7,095 million in 2019, which was just over one-third (36.5%) of its profit for the year. Unfortunately there is no prior year information given, so it is difficult to assess Runnabout's dividend policy.

Similarly, there is no historic information presented for Dokbyke, but it is interesting to note that Dokbyke paid out a higher proportion of its profits (62.6%).

Conclusion

As stated above, the dividend decision involves striking a balance between paying dividends and retaining profit to finance expansion. The evidence would suggest that Runnabout has that balance about right.

3 Evaluate the corporate governance structure at Runnabout (P3).

Runnabout is the parent company of the Runnabout Group, it is a national micromobility hire company based in the country of Geeland. It listed on the Geeland stock exchange in 2010 and so therefore needs to adhere to the Geeland Code of Corporate Governance. As the listing was a reasonable time ago, it is likely that they have developed a process for corporate governance. The Geeland Stock Exchange is active and well regulated.

Corporate governance guidelines exist so that the needs of shareholders are met. Monitoring exists so that directors are kept 'in check' and minimising any problems arising from the agency relationship between principals (shareholders) and agents (directors).

We are not told about the shareholdings of any of the directors, but presumably some of the board own some of the shares, this should reduce the agency issue at Runnabout. Assuming the board were not to act in the best interests of the shareholders they would be jeopardising their own interests. If this is the case there would be a reduction in the need (and costs) of monitoring the board.

Applying corporate guidelines for good governance, the following are considerations worth noting.

Board Balance

A board should be balanced in terms of skills, experience and diversity. Such a structure will help enable the Runnabout board to deal with strategic and operational issues.

CEO Mei Yee has a long history working in logistics, having worked for a courier company as a senior logistics manager for 16 years prior to joining Runnabout. Chief Financial Officer Geo Pataros is a professionally qualified accountant and has finance experience in the micromobility industry. Director of Operations, Alan Peters, has significant experience in traffic operation within a city from his time at Western City Council and is Runnabout's longest serving board member. Shaun McDougall is the IT Director and has experience at various major quoted companies including gaming companies prior to joining Runnabout's board. Pat Olly is Human Resource Director, this a good sign for Runnabout as they employ around 15,000 staff in a wide variety of roles across Geeland. She seems to have a good range of HR experience across a variety of organisations.

They have all served on the board for varying lengths of time, some are in their first year, and so may still be learning about the company and the day to day operations.

There is one area of business operations that does not appear to be well served by the Board, this is legal affairs. Given the nature of the industry that Runnabout operate in, which is basically transport, and the emphasis on background checks (particularly in IT) on their employees because of their access to confidential data this could be an area of concern.

Runnabout have three Non-Executive Directors (NEDs), all of whom are stated as being independent and bring further useful experience to the board. Marco Palermo is a qualified accountant, Juliana Leung brings further transport expertise, and Patrick Chiu has medical experience and further financial expertise. The NEDs have all been on the board for more than 3 years, so don't have any issues with time served independence. Currently there is no reason to question their independence, but this may change in the unseen.

Under corporate governance guidelines a board should be balanced in terms of the number of executive and NED roles. There should be the same number of NEDs as executives (excluding the Chair), that is executive directors should not outnumber the NEDs. In addition, in order to ensure the NEDs represent the interests of the shareholders they should be independent. A smaller company should have at least two independent NEDs.

As Runnabout has three NEDs versus the five directors (this excludes the chair) the main criteria is not met. The NEDs will hopefully be able to provide sound business advice to aid the running of the company. NEDs are also meant to challenge the executives and act on behalf of the shareholders. This is less likely to happen at Runnabout if there is any reason why they are not independent.

CEO and Chair roles

These roles have been split at Runnabout which is compliant with most countries' corporate governance guidance.

The Chair's role is to run the Board; the CEO's role is to run the company. Placing both in one person's hands may give them too much power. Given that Runnabout have insufficient NEDs to keep such power 'in check' it would be more important.

The Chair is the representative of the shareholders – they should be able to communicate any matters of concern to the Chair. Jack Avery is Runnabout's Chair, and appears to have been independent on appointment, although we have no information about Capital City Buses and any potential business relationship with Runnabout.

Committees

There are three committees mentioned at Runnabout – Audit, Risk and Remuneration – although that does not mean others do not exist.

All committees make use of NEDs under most Corporate Governance Codes. The compulsory committees are: Remuneration, Nominations and Audit committee, so ideally Runnabout should also have a Nomination committee too.

The Audit committee should have at least three, or in the case of smaller companies two, independent non-executive directors. The chair of the board should not be on the audit committee. In smaller companies the company chair may be a member of, but not chair, the committee in addition to the independent non-executive directors, provided he or she was considered independent on appointment as Chair. At least one member of the audit committee should have recent and relevant financial experience.

Runnabout's audit committee could satisfy the criteria, but it would depend on the definition of small, because Jack Avery is on the committee it does not comply with guidance for larger organisations. Runnabout do have the necessary financial experience as Marco Palermo is on the committee. It would be better if Jack Avery were to step down from the audit committee and be replaced by Patrick Chiu.

The Remuneration committee should have at least three, or in the case of smaller companies two, independent non-executive directors. In addition the company chair may also be a member of, but not chair, the committee if he or she was considered independent on appointment as chair. For Runnabout, either criteria could be met, Jack Avery is again on this committee, but we do not know who is chair of this committee, if it was Jack then Runnabout would not comply with the criteria. In this case, it is in line with guidelines for Jack to be on the committee (provided he was independent on appointment as chair of the board).

The Nomination committee is usually expected to have a majority of NEDs, so again could feasibly be in existence at Runnabout.

The risk committee is a useful committee to have and will give investors more confidence that Runnabout take risk seriously, there are no guidelines for the composition of this committee.

We can see that the three NEDs are all on 2 committees each, with Jack involved in all three. Based on this the NEDs should not have too much power or a workload so excessive that they cannot carry out their roles adequately. Although Jack may have, as he is on all three committees as well as chairing the overall board. Jack should not be chair of any of these committees, or even be on the audit committee.

Overall

The biggest concern would be the lack of Legal director, the lack of NEDs and Jack's position on the audit committee should also be reviewed.

We must also be prepared for additional information in the unseen to present other potential problems, such as a key board member wishing to leave, or independence issues.

4 Discuss Runnabout's exposure to risk and suggest suitable mitigations (other than risks included on the Principal Risks extract in the annual report).

Reputation risk

Any mistakes made by Runnabout, from board level to the front line labour force could lead to reputation damage, whether that is from damaged hoverboards not being removed from service in a timely manner or an ill-advised tweet on social media. Reputation damage could also be caused by improper labour practices, fraud or even cyber-attacks.

Mitigation

Good HR practices and training, sufficient staff and realistic targets will help, as will a good control environment (tone from the top). Careful background history checks on employees handling sensitive data will help ensure that Runnabout do not breach any legislation or allow inappropriate access to their data.

Competitive environment

Despite the exclusivity that Runnabout currently have, there are still other forms competing with them from scooters and bikes, but also to walking and running.

Mitigation

At present in terms of speed and convenience Runnabout appear to have the balance better than other micromobility options, but they must remain vigilant to changes in tech, regulation and consumer behaviour.

Political risk

Possibly the single biggest risk in the case study. If the government changes parties or there are changes in legislation about the need to wear helmets, if hoverboards are allowed on the pavement, if there are other hoverboard hire firms allowed to operate in the cities of Geeland, it would have a significant impact on Runnabout's operations.

Mitigation

Continued good working relationships with the governments and a good safety record.

Bank Facility

Runnabout has a G$62,475 million loan, and while it doesn't appear to be in financial difficulty at present, having a positive position with the bank in both 2018 & 2019, if they need to refinance they need to be aware of potential risk that the rates may rise from the current level of around 9% this is already up significantly on last year (5.2%).

Mitigation

A good relationship with the bank to make sure that they are aware of any issues and the steps being taken. Good controls to help protect the business and clear planning to show how they plan to remain competitive will assist with that relationship.

Litigation

Runnabout could be at risk of litigation from staff or customers. Staff through the health and safety in the workplace, customers from a variety of reasons for example injury or loss of personal data.

Mitigation

Recruitment and good HR procedures will help, such as the background checks on employees who access users' data. Runnabout also have insurance against any claims.

Health and safety

Runnabout has 15,000 employees, the physical nature of some of the work involved particularly moving and fixing hoverboards could increase these risks. Any issues in the workplace could lead to litigation against Runnabout if they are not compliant with legislation.

Mitigation

Runnabout must make sure they are aware of the legislation in Geeland and compliant with it too. A focus on HR, and the work done by Pat Olly and her team will help, but the potential of increased legal expertise could also help further. Runnabout also have insurance against any claims.

Disruption

The "last mile" of the journey is an ever increasing problem in a time poor society that won't (or is reluctant to) walk the final mile. Hoverboards could be disrupted by something safer and just as quick (potentially not quicker as it would probably require safety accessories such as a helmet).

Mitigation

Runnabout has been at the forefront of micromobility, so it would seem logical that Runnabout will be considering new inventions that could replace hoverboards either by inventing themselves or acquisition of a new start-up.

Environmental risk

Anything that consumes the world's resources has an environmental impact and something with a battery like the hoverboard, depending on how it is decommissioned/deposed of could have a significant adverse impact on the environment. Broken hoverboards could be discarded by disgruntled customers. A 6 month life cycle for a hoverboard seems quite a burden on the environment.

Mitigation

Runnabout includes in its values "minimise the environmental footprint of its micromobility solutions" which shows they have environmental considerations at the heart of what they do. Policy handbooks and regular training updates could help reinforce this focus for their staff.

Currency risk

In terms of currency risk, as Runnabout makes sales entirely within their own country they do not appear to be subject to any transaction risk from sales, but their main supplier is based in Deeland, so there could be transaction risk on purchases. They will be subject to economic risk, as the economy of Geeland will influence disposable income and visitors to Geeland.

Mitigation

Diversification geographically across Geeland will help, but potentially diversification overseas would reduce reliance on the Geeland economy. Hedging could be used on purchases from Minnerring.

5   Identify possible strategies for growth for Runnabout.

Ansoff's matrix is a useful model that summarises the possible growth options for an organisation. It does this by looking at two variables, the market served and the product offered, and categories each of these as either existing or new.

A specific application to Runnabout would be as follows:

Market penetration – existing product, existing market

This strategy is essentially about increasing market share in a market Runnabout already operates in (cities in Geeland) with an existing product (hoverboard sharing). Runnabout would be looking to increase its market share; given that no other organisations have been granted a licence to offer such services to date, Runnabout has 100% market share, and would therefore be looking to increase the size of the market.

Given that Geeland has a population of over 1 billion people, there must be many towns and cities which are not currently served by Runnabout services. Feasibility studies could be carried out to identify suitable locations; this should include local geography (the city needs to be relatively flat), and the local authority needs to be receptive to the idea of granting Runnabout a licence to operate. This would then increase the company's presence in Geeland to more than the current 15 locations.

Alternatively, Runnabout could embark on a marketing campaign to attract more users to its current locations. This would mean increasing the utilisation of existing assets. The campaign would have two principal aims; firstly, to attract micromobility users to switch from an alternative means of travelling 'the last mile' i.e. to persuade them to use hoverboards instead of bikes or electric scooters. Secondly, Runnabout would want to attract more of Geeland's travelling public to see micromobility as part of their overall journey.

Product development (existing market, new product)

A product development strategy is one of bringing a new product to an existing market.

The Geeland market for micromobility is essentially the market that Runnabout operates in, but currently only in 1 form – hoverboards. Product development would therefore mean the company diversifying into an alternative means of transport, such as bike sharing or electric scooters.

Bike sharing is an area that the company has experience of; indeed, it was only 4 years ago that it withdrew from this segment of the market, and so it should not be too difficult to offer such services again. The basic key skills will still be present in its employee base, and the concept is the same as offering hoverboard sharing services.

Whilst bike sharing is a competitive market, it still has the potential to be lucrative; an analysis of Dokbyke's latest financial statements shows revenue growth and profit margins that were higher than that of Runnabout in 2019. In addition, Runnabout has knowledge of more towns and cities than Dokbyke (15 compared to 6) which would mean that it is better positioned to enjoy possible economies of scale.

Electric scooters is another form of micromobility that it could diversify into. Again, some key skills are already present in Runnabout, such as putting in place docking stations that can recharge each machine. The technological platform for offering such services i.e. an app for use on smart phones would need very little adapting from what is currently in place for hoverboards.

Alternatively, Runnabout might try to develop new forms of micromobility, such as roller blades that can be picked up and dropped off at designated points. However, this is likely to be higher risk, given that there is no established market demand for anything truly innovative.

Market development (existing product, new market)

Market development means finding a new market to sell an existing product to. This could be in the form of targeting a new segment of the population in Geeland, such as looking to attract an age bracket that currently is not being serviced by Runnabout. For example, it might be possible to start allowing users below the age of 18 to use hoverboards, as long as they have a lower maximum speed, greater stability, and the child has to be accompanied by an adult. This would therefore attract families to possibly start using Runnabout's services.

Alternatively, it may be that older people are put off using hoverboards due to their perceived lack of stability. This could be addressed by introducing new boards which have an upright handle to hold onto and, again, a lower restricted speed. Or even a combination of a handle and a seat, much as a typical mobility scooter would have. It would be more cost effective for a user to hire one as it is needed rather than purchase one outright.

However, the greatest potential for growth is likely to come from expanding outside of Geeland. Runnabout suffers from lack of diversity in this respect; its operations are wholly dependent on both the level of demand in Geeland and the approval of local authorities for hoverboards to be used on pavements. There must surely be other developed countries that would welcome initiatives that will reduce pollution and congestion in urban areas – again, feasibility studies should be carried out to identify and evaluate suitable locations.

Runnabout could emphasise its ability to service such 'last mile' needs in persuading foreign governments to grant it a licence to operate, using its large database of registered users as proof, and also the employment possibilities that might be generated, as local mechanics would surely be required to maintain the fleet of boards.

Diversification (new product, new market)

This strategy carries the greatest degree of risk, in that both product and market would be new to Runnabout simultaneously.

Diversification could be into related areas, such as other elements of the overall supply chain for hoverboards (perhaps Runnabout could start to manufacture its own boards as opposed to sourcing them from Minnerring Robotics? This could be deemed a form of vertical integration.

On the other hand, Runnabout could look at the subject of transport in a broader way. For example, it could open a chain of hoverboard or bike shops, becoming a retailer of goods instead of a service provider.

Alternatively it could diversify in completely unrelated areas; this is almost limitless in terms of possibilities, such as becoming a bank or operating a chain of coffee bars.

Exercise 2 – Runnabout: Ratio Analysis

Workings – Runnabout

All in G$m		2019		2018	
Revenue growth		85,211 to 97,943	14.9%		No information
Operating profit growth		26,500 to 31,897	20.4%		No information
Capital employed	Loans + Equity	62,475 + 51,491	113,966	55,475 + 39,143	94,618
Return on Capital Employed (ROCE)	(Operating profit / Capital Employed) × 100%	(31,897 / 113,966) × 100%	28.0%	(26,500 / 94,618) × 100%	28.0%
Asset turnover	Revenue / Capital Employed	97,943 / 113,966	0.86	85,211 / 94,618	0.90
Operating profit (%)	(Operating profit / Revenue) × 100%	(31,897 / 97,943) × 100%	32.6%	(26,500 / 85,211) × 100%	31.1%
Gross profit (%)	(Gross profit / Revenue) × 100%	((97,943 – 39,908) / 97,943) × 100%	59.3%	((85,211 – 34,323) / 85,211 × 100%	59.7%
Return on equity (ROE)	(Profit for the year / Equity) × 100%	(19,443 / 51,491) × 100%	37.8%	(16,725 / 39,143) × 100%	42.7%

Workings – Dokbyke

All in G$m		2019	2018		
Revenue growth		23,859 to 28,403	19.0%		No information
Operating profit growth		8,741 to 10,573	21.0%		No information
Capital employed	Loans + Equity	11,993 + 8,660	20,653	14,424 + 6,029	20,453
Return on Capital Employed (ROCE)	(Operating profit / Capital Employed) × 100%	(10,573 / 20,653) × 100%	51.2%	(8,741 / 20,453) × 100%	42.7%
Asset turnover	Revenue / Capital Employed	28,403 / 20,653	1.38	23,859 / 20,453	1.17
Operating profit (%)	(Operating profit / Revenue) × 100%	(10,573 / 28,403) × 100%	37.2%	(8,741 / 23,859) × 100%	36.6%
Gross profit (%)	(Gross profit / Revenue) × 100%	((28,403 – 9,788) / 28,403) × 100%	65.5%	((23,859 – 7,624) / 23,859) × 100%	68.0%
Return on equity (ROE)	(Profit for the year / Equity) × 100%	(7,026 / 8,660) × 100%	81.1%	(5,508 / 6,029) × 100%	91.4%

Commentary:

Initial thoughts – relative size of the companies, and different businesses

Runnabout is a much bigger company than Dokbyke. Its revenue in 2019 was more than three times higher (G$ 97,943 million versus G$ 28,403 million) and its profit for the year was just under three times bigger (G$ 19,443 million versus G$ 7,026 million).

Also, the two businesses offer very different services. Although both are classified as micromobility companies, Runnabout has a monopoly in Geeland as the only hoverboard-sharing company while Dokbyke is one of several bicycle-sharing companies.

Therefore any comparison of the financial results and position of the two companies might be of limited use.

Runnabout performance analysis

Runnabout has achieved impressive growth in revenue and operating profit in 2019. Its ROCE has stayed constant at a healthy 28.0% in 2018 and 2019.

Breaking down the ROCE into asset turnover and operating profit margin shows a slight improvement in operating profit margin and a slight worsening of asset turnover. Without more information, it is impossible to say whether this is the start of a significant new trend or just a short-term fluctuation. Similarly it is impossible to read too much into the slight fall in gross profit margin.

Return on Equity (ROE) fell sharply in 2019, largely because of the rise in retained earnings (equity) rather than any problem with profitability. The rise in share price towards the end of the year (page 20 of the pre-seen) suggests that shareholders are not particularly concerned by the lower ROE.

Overall, Runnabout seems to have performed well in 2019.

Dokbyke performance analysis

Although Runnabout seems to have performed well in 2019, Dokbyke has outperformed Runnabout in every single metric! (higher growth rate, higher ROCE, higher profit margins etc).

This is surprising given that Runnabout enjoys a monopoly in its niche of the micromobility market while Dokbyke is one of several competitors in its sector.

If the bicycle-sharing sector in general is outperforming hoverboard-sharing, it seems odd that Runnabout changed its entire business model in 2016 to replace bicycles with hoverboards. More information on the whole bicycle-sharing sector (rather than just one company in the sector) would help us to assess whether Runnabout should diversify or change its strategy.

Exercise 3 – Runnabout: SWOT analysis

Strengths

- Quoted company, therefore access to capital markets if further finance needed

- Share price has doubled in last 6 months, indicating positive view of investing community

- Revenue has grown by 15% in the last year

- Operating profit has increased by 20%, indicating possible economies of scale

- Presence in 15 cities in Geeland

- $2.3 bn of cash in the bank

- Supplier arrangement with Minnerring, which makes robust hoverboards

- Over 30m registered users

- Team of mobile mechanics to carry out prompt repairs/reposition fleet – should result in effective asset use

- Board has a history of identifying successfully when to change strategy (bikes to e-bikes to hoverboards)

- Based in Geeland, which is a prosperous country and relatively flat

- Use of technology (mobile phone app) to book hires is easy to use and appeals to millennials

- Payment by debit/credit card means cash receipt is almost instant, therefore better for cash operating cycle

- Average operating profit per ride is $3.61, or 62.2% of revenue

- Software restricts maximum speed, and so should minimise risk of accident

- Use of a remote hot backup site should reduce risk of operations being disrupted due to IT system failure

- Presence of seemingly useful Internal Audit department reduces control risks.

Weaknesses

- High business risk – only focus is on hoverboard sharing
- Fairly high gearing levels may make it difficult to raise further debt finance
- Average life of a hoverboard is 6 months, so constant need for replacement
- Beta factors suggest higher than average systematic risk (both geared and ungeared > 1).

Opportunities

- Expansion into further cities in Geeland (country has a population of over 1 bn people, so presumably many cities without Runnabout presence)
- Expansion into foreign countries of hoverboard sharing
- Expand into other forms of mobility sharing – bikes, scooters
- Act as a consultant on transportation services to local authorities
- Diversify into other uses for hoverboards e.g. children's parties, guided tours
- Acquisition of/merger with other mobility sharing companies e.g. Dokbyke
- Sponsorship of IT courses at university, similar to that of Dokbyke.

Threats

- Governments (local, national) may ban hoverboards from pavements
- A weakening G$ could result in higher costs when buying hoverboards from Deeland
- Hack of IT systems – sensitive data is held about each registered user, including debit/credit card details
- Rider/pedestrian/other is injured as a result of poor riding/software fault – could result in litigation against Runnabout
- Authorities may start granting licences to competitors
- Authorities may insist on riders wearing helmets, which resulted in reduced demand for bike sharing
- Rider is injured due to hoverboard over-heating and bursting into flames, resulting in litigation/loss of reputation
- Insurance covers **valid** hires only – Runnabout may not be covered in event a hire is made to under 18 or no drivers' licence
- Extended disruption to mobile phone services
- National government decides to restrict size of docking stations.

Exam day techniques

Chapter learning objectives

- To develop a carefully planned and thought through strategy to cope with the three hours of exam time

1 Exam day strategy

Once you have studied the pre-seen, learnt the three subject syllabi thoroughly and practised lots of exercises and mocks, you should be well prepared for the exam.

However, it is still important to have a carefully planned and thought through strategy to cope with those three hours of exam time.

This chapter takes you through some of the key skills to master to ensure all your careful preparation does not go to waste.

2 Importance of time management

Someone once referred to case study exams as "the race against time" and it's difficult to imagine a more accurate description. Being able to do what the examiner is wanting is only half of the battle; being able to deliver it in the time available is another matter altogether. This is even more important than in previous exams you may have faced because each section in the real exam is now timed and that once that time is up you will be moved on. Case study is not like a traditional exam where you can go back to a question if you get extra inspiration or feel you have some time left over. You have to complete each task within the time stated.

For this reason, time management is a key skill required to pass the Case Study Examination.

Successful time management requires two things:

- A tailored time plan – one that plays to your personal strengths and weaknesses; and

- Discipline in order to stick to it!

Time robbers

There are a number of ways in which time can be wasted or not used effectively in the Case Study Examination. An awareness of these will help to ensure you don't waste time in your exam.

Inactive reading

The first part of each task must be spent actively reading, processing the information and considering the impact on the organisation, how the issues link together and what could be done to resolve them. You may not have time to have a second detailed read and so these thoughts must be captured first time around.

Too much time spent on presentation

You will be writing your answer in software with some similarities to Microsoft Word however the only functions available are

- Cut

- Copy

- Paste

- Undo

- Redo

- Bold

- Italic

- Underline

The temptation to make various words bold or italics or underlined, is very hard to resist. But, resist you must! There are little, if any, marks available for having a response that is well presented, and these finer details will be worth nothing at all. Good presentation could involve writing in paragraphs, which makes the progression from one line of thought to the next much easier and subheadings within answers. CIMA wouldn't actually award marks for that, but a well-structured argument demonstrates greater understanding.

Being a perfectionist

Students can often spend such a long time pondering about what to write that over the course of a 3 hour exam, over half of it is spent staring into space.

As you are sitting a computer exam you not only spend time pondering, but also have the ability to delete so can change your mind several times before settling on the right word combinations. Just focus on getting your points down and don't worry about whether they could have been phrased better.

Although do bear in mind that the marker has to be able to read and understand your answer, so do write in clear English.

Too much detail on earlier parts of the requirement

As we've said earlier, not finishing answers is a key reason for failing the Case Study Examination. One of the main reasons why students fail to finish a section is a lack of discipline when writing about an issue. They feel they have to get all of their points down rather than selecting the better points and moving on. If a task requires you to discuss three different areas it is vital that you cover all parts adequately.

Too much correction

Often students can reread paragraphs three or more times before they move on to writing the next part of their answer. Instead, try to leave the read through until the final few minutes of the task and try to correct as many obvious errors as possible. The CIMA marker will be reading and marking your script on screen and it is harder to read and understand the points you are making if there are many typing errors. Having said this, typing errors are never directly penalised; as long as the marker can understand the point you are trying to make, the odd mistake doesn't matter.

3 Assimilation of information

One of the most challenging things to deal with in a case study examination is the volume of information which you have available. This is particularly difficult when you have both pre-seen and unseen information to manage and draw from. It is important that you refer to relevant pre-seen information in your responses as well as incorporating the unseen information.

The key things that you need to do to assimilate the information effectively and efficiently are:

- Read about and identify each event

- Consider what the issue is

- Evaluate the impact of the issue. Who is affected, by how much are they affected and what would happen if no action was taken?

- Determine the most useful and relevant exhibits from the pre-seen

Capturing all of your thoughts and ideas at this stage can be difficult and time consuming.

The following section on planning your answer will show you how to do this effectively without wasting time or effort.

4 Planning your answers

In section 2 of this chapter we saw how important it was to manage your time in the exam to ensure you're able to complete all of the necessary stages in the preparation of your answer.

One important aspect of your exam is planning your answer. Sitting the Case Study Exam is not as straight forward as turning up, reading the requirements, and then writing your answer.

If you do attempt to write without any form of content plan, your response will lack direction and a logical flow, it won't fully address the key points required and any recommendations will lack solid justification. It is for this reason that time should be specifically allocated to planning the content of your answers.

Given the preparation you've done before the exam, reading the unseen can often feel like a firework display is happening in your brain; each new piece of information you read about triggers a series of thoughts and ideas.

The planning process must therefore begin as soon as you start reading the unseen information. Every second counts within the case study exam and so it's important to use all of your time effectively by capturing the thoughts as they come to you.

To make sure the time spent now is of use to you throughout the task, you will need to consider carefully how best to document your thoughts. You will be provided with an on-screen notes page ('scratchpad') as well as a wipe-clean laminated notes page and marker pen. Any method you adopt to plan must be concise whilst still allowing you to capture all of your ideas and see the bigger picture in terms of how the issues interrelate with one another (see additional guidance below). Furthermore, the method must suit you! Everyone is different and what might work for one person could be a disaster for another. For example, some people prefer to work with lists, others with mind maps.

Most people find that some form of central planning sheet (to enable the bigger picture to be seen) is best. How you prepare the central planning sheet is a matter of personal preference and we've given illustrations of two different methods below. Practise each one to find out which you prefer and then tailor it further to settle on something that works for you.

Method 1 – The ordered list

This process is ideally suited to people who prefer lists and structure.

Step 1:

- Begin by reading everything in the task exhibit

- Ensure you have identified all aspects of the task and then write this on the left hand side of your planning sheet

Step 2:

- Read everything in the trigger exhibit, making notes next to the relevant task

Step 3:

- Review your list to identify any linkages to information provided in the pre-seen and note next to the task on your planning sheet

Step 4:

- Brainstorm any technical knowledge you can use in responding to the task and note this on your planning sheet

Illustration 1 – Planning

On Monday morning your boss arrived in work full of enthusiasm for a new business venture he had thought of over the weekend. This was in response to a conversation that had taken place at Friday night drinks when the CEO expressed concern that she felt the business was stagnating and needed some new products to rekindle customer interest.

Your boss needed to harness his ideas and put together an outline plan for a mid-morning coffee meeting with the CEO. Typically, the idea had germinated without sufficient thought and you were asked to consider the critical factors that needed to be considered in launching the new product and write a briefing document for the meeting.

Requirement:

Prepare a plan for your briefing document.

Solution

Critical factors	Goals and objectives	Skills and experience	Finance	Marketing and sales
New product	Matches mission and objectives?	Experience in manufacturing?	Available finance?	Advertising
	Strengths?	Available labour?	Investment?	Social media
			Working capital?	Website?
Technical content?		SAF?	Debt v equity? Investment appraisal techniques?	

Method 2 – The extended mind map

This process is ideally suited to those who prefer pictures and diagrams to trigger their thoughts.

Step 1:

- Read the unseen information and identify the key tasks required

- As you read, write each task in a "bubble" on your planning sheet.

Step 2:

- Keep adding each new part of the task you identify to your sheet. At the end you should have a page with a number of bubbles dotted about.

Step 3:

- Review your bubbles to identify any linkages to the trigger information or pre-seen exhibits. Add any relevant information to your planning sheet in a bubble attached to the appropriate part of the task.

Step 4:

- Review the task bubbles and brainstorm any relevant knowledge which you can use in responding to the task. Add this to bubbles attached to the task.

With detailed information provided in the exam it would be very likely that your brain would think of a wide range of ideas which, if left uncaptured, would be forgotten as quickly as you thought of them.

This is where mind mapping comes in handy. You would not of course need to draw one as neat as this and feel free to add colours or graphics to help your thought processes.

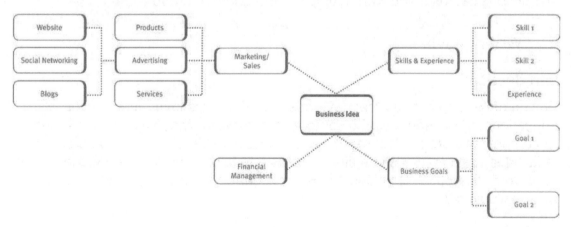

Have a go!

Why not try putting your thoughts on the previous illustration into a mind map like the one above?

Some additional guidance

(1) This is perhaps the hardest part of the exam; as soon as you tell your brain it needs to come up with some ideas, it very often refuses to cooperate! Practice makes perfect so working through the exercises in Chapter 7 and attempting mock exams will really help your brain to deliver ideas when you need it to.

(2) Don't simply view technical models as something that must be included to tick a box if explicitly requested in the requirements. Instead use the models to help analyse the issues, suggest solutions or generate ideas. They were developed to be useful!

(3) If you start looking at one of the task requirements and are stuck for ideas, don't waste time staring into space. Move on to the next part of the task (but not onto the next task itself as you won't be able to return) and you'll find the creative juices soon start flowing.

5 Communication skills

The Case Study examinations aim to test a wide range of skills and you may be required to communicate in many different ways to various different audiences, each with different information needs. How well you communicate will be directly linked to the marks earned – clear, appropriate communication will always score better than confused, irrelevant or vague ideas.

In Strategic Case study, the examiners do not tend to ask for specific formats for a response – an email, letter, report etc. Instead, you should simply type your answer in the box provided, getting straight into the answer to the instructions set, as if you were typing out the body of a report.

6 Writing style

Introduction

Writing style is something that develops over time. It is influenced by your education and experiences. To some it comes easily, they enjoy words – but remember, you are not looking to win any prizes in literature. It's about putting facts, ideas and opinions in a clear, concise, logical fashion. Some students get very worried about their writing styles. As a general rule you should try to write as you would talk.

Logical flow

A typical point starts with a statement of fact, either given in the case or derived from analysis – 'what?'

This can then be followed by an interpretation – 'so what?'

This can then lead to an implication – 'now what?', or 'what next?'

For example:

(1)   What? – The net relevant cash flow for the project is positive.

(2)   So what? – Suggesting we should go ahead with the project.

(3)   Now what? – Arrange board meeting to discuss strategic implications.

A similar structure can be obtained using the Socratic approach – what, why, how?

- So what?

- Why should we use it?

- How does it work?

Who is reading the response?

Failure to pitch the level correctly will inevitably result in failure to communicate your ideas effectively, since the reader will either be swamped with complexity, or bored with blandness. The recipients of the report should also dictate the level of tact required.

Tactless	Tactful
The directors have clearly made errors	There were other options open to the board that, with hindsight, would have been beneficial
The marketing director is responsible for this disastrous change in strategy	The board should consider where this went wrong? It would appear that the marketing department may have made some mistakes

This has to be considered carefully. If, for argument's sake, the question asked for an evaluation of a director's proposal, it would cost marks if the candidate glossed over the proposal's weaknesses in order to avoid upsetting the Boss. The "real world" analogy can be taken too far.

It should be made clear that candidates will never be penalised for rejecting or disagreeing with a proposal made by the CEO or any other senior colleague if doing so results in a strong and relevant answer to the requirement.

Making your response easy to read

To ensure that the marker finds your answers accessible and easy to read, you should try to do the following:

- Use short words, short sentences, short phrases and short paragraphs. If you are adopting the 'what, so what, what now' approach, then you could have a paragraph containing three sentences. The next point can then be a new paragraph, also containing three sentences.

- Use the correct words to explain what you mean! For example, students often get confused between:

  - recommendations (what they should do – actions) and options (what they could do – possibilities).

  - objectives (what we want to achieve – the destination) and strategies (how we intend to achieve them – the route).

- Avoid using vague generalisations. Too often students will comment that an issue will "impact" on profit rather than being specific about whether profit will increase or decrease (or even better still, trying to quantify by how much). Other common phrases which are too vague include "communicate with" (you need to say specifically what should be discussed) and "look in to" (how should an option be looked in to?)

- Avoid unnecessary repetition. This can either be of information from the exam paper (pre-seen or unseen), of discussion within the report (in particular between what is said in one section and another) or can relate to the words that you use. Some students fall into the trap of thinking that writing a professional report means simply writing more words to say the same thing! The issue is quality not quantity.

  For example, compare the following:

  - 'I, myself, personally' OR 'I'

  - 'export overseas' OR 'export'

  - 'green in colour' OR 'green'

- Watch your spelling – this may seem a small and unimportant point, but poor spelling makes a document seem sloppy and may convey an impression that the content is as loose as the general appearance! Having said this, do not worry about the occasional spelling mistake or typo in your answer; CIMA will not penalise you, provided they can understand what you are trying to say.

- Recommendations – be decisive – do not 'sit on the fence' or ask for more information. Make a clear recommendation based on the information you have and justify why you have chosen that course of action.

Exercise 1

This exercise will get you thinking about what makes a well written script. The technical content of the requirement is not relevant – we are focusing on writing style and flow.

The risk committee of X plc met to discuss a report by its risk manager. The report focused on a number of risks that applied to a chemicals factory recently acquired in another country.

She explained that the new risks related to the security of the new factory in respect of burglary, the supply of one of the key raw materials that experienced fluctuations in world supply and also an environmental risk.

The environmental risk was with respect to the possibility of poisonous emissions from the new factory. The CEO who chaired the risk committee, said that the factory was important to him for two reasons. First, he said it was strategically important to the company. Second, it was important because his own bonuses depended upon it. He said that he knew from the report what the risks were, but that he wanted somebody to explain to him what strategies they could use to manage the risks. 'I don't get any bonus at all until we reach a high level of output from the factory,' he said. 'So I don't care what the risks are, we will have to manage them.'

You have been asked to outline strategies that can be used to manage risk and identify, with reasons, an appropriate strategy for each of the three risks facing the new venture.

Requirement:

Consider these two responses and note the positive and negative aspects of each.

Answer 1

Introduction

Risk can be managed using the following strategies.

- **Transfer** the risk to another organisation for example by buying insurance. This is usually cost effective where the probability of the risk is low but the impact is potentially high.

- **Avoid** the risk altogether by withdrawing completely from the risky activity. This is done where the risk is high probability and high frequency and so it is too costly to reduce the risk sufficiently.

- **Reduce** the risk by implementing controls or by diversification.

- **Accept** the risk without taking any further steps to mitigate it. For this to be acceptable the frequency and the impact of the risk must place the risk within the risk appetite of the company.

Risk of burglary

It is usual to insure against burglary an example of the transfer strategy. This is because of the high impact of burglary.

It is also usual to put safeguards in place such as security guards because of the probability of burglary. This is an example of risk reduction.

Raw materials supply fluctuation

Depending on the cost benefit analysis the company could chose to transfer the risk by entering into forward contracts to purchase the materials.

There will be a cost associated with this and it will lower but not remove the risk associated with supply and price fluctuations. They may choose to accept the risk as part of the operational risk associated with their industry.

Environmental risk

The company should take reasonable steps to reduce the chance poisonous emissions. It should use appropriate technology and controls to reduce the risk.

Risks cannot be completely eliminated so if the poisonous emissions could give rise to significant costs it should also purchase insurance and transfer the risk.

Answer 2

Risk is managed by this:

(1) Identify the risk. This is by brainstorming all the things that the risk can be.

(2) Risk assessment. We won't know this properly until afterwards.

(3) Risk Profiling. This is decided on consequences and impact.

(4) Risk quantification. This can be average loss or it can be largest loss.

(5) Risk consolidation which will depend on the risk appetite and diversification.

The risks at the factory are:

• The main risk at the factory is environmental risk. You can't do anything about this risk because global warming is because of everyone.

• The big risk is that the CEO is "I don't care what the risks are" this will need to have the risk awareness embedded in and the tone at the top.

• The other risk is that the CEO could manipulate the output levels to get his bonus. This needs to be looked at seriously because he is also on the risk committee and the remuneration committee and he is not independent and that should be a NED.

---

7 Summary

You should have an appreciation of some of the issues you may encounter in the exam and some possible techniques to overcome these.

Next steps:

(1) In the next two chapters we will present the unseen and guide you through the process of producing an answer. It is worth ensuring you can log on to the Pearson Vue site now and make sure you have registered for the practice case study exam. It is advisable to familiarise yourself with the software as much as possible.

(2) As you are about to embark on a full attempt at the question tutorial exam it is a good time to revisit previous chapters and ensure you are comfortable with all of the material so far before proceeding.

Test your understanding answers

 Exercise 1

The first solution has several positive aspects:

- Brief introduction linking to requirement

- Overview of model with explanation and clear examples

- Specific points from scenario addressed

- Headings clearly signpost the answer

- Appropriate language

There are some areas which could be improved:

- Specific reference to the company name

- More explicit use of the information from the scenario

The second solution is not as strong as the first. Some of the main criticisms:

- Main options available are not clearly explained

- No attempt to introduce the answer

- Inappropriate language for a formal report/response

- Lack of tact regarding the CEO – the intended audience!!

As a piece of writing there is not much to say from a positive perspective except:

- Clear structure

- Writing is concise (but probably a bit too brief)

May and August 2020 real exam variant 1 – walkthrough

Chapter learning objectives

- To gain experience trying to answer a case study exam.

1   The aim of a walkthrough

The aim of this chapter is to give you a chance to practise many of the techniques you have been shown in previous chapters of this study text. This should help you to understand the various thought processes needed to complete the full three hour examination. It is important that you work through this chapter at a steady pace.

Don't rush on to the next stage until you have properly digested the information, followed the guidance labelled 'Stop and Think!' and made your own notes. This will give you more confidence than simply reading the model solutions. You should refer to the unseen produced in the previous chapter as you proceed through these exercises.

The following chapter will then guide you through the suggested solutions and marking key.

2   First screen

The opening screen of the exam shows you how many sub-tasks you have to deal with and how to allocate your time within tasks:

Section (task)	Time for section (minutes)	Number of answer screens	Number of sub-tasks	% time to spend on each sub-task
1	60	1	2	(a) 60% (b) 40%
2	60	1	2	(a) 50% (b) 50%
3	60	1	3	(a) 40% (b) 30% (c) 30%

The exam software will prevent you from spending more than 60 minutes on task 2, say, but you need to ensure that this is split 30 minutes on sub-task (a) and 30 minutes on sub-task (b)

3 Task 1

Understanding the context

The first screen of task 1 reveals that Runnabout is concerned about hoverboards being hacked:

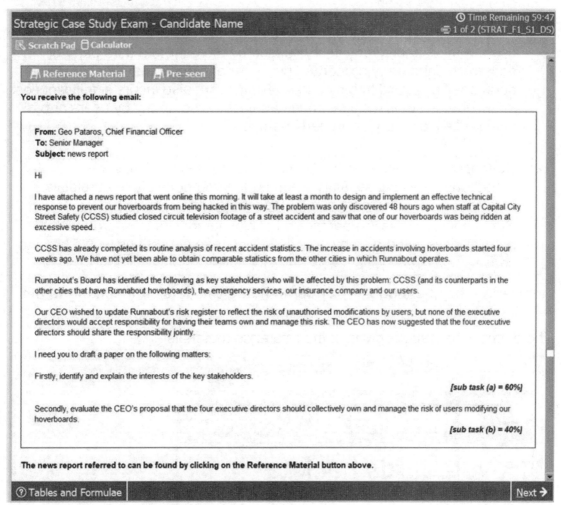

Stop and think!

(1) Start thinking about the relevant information in the pre-seen. It's very important that your responses are applied to the scenario. For example, how much can you remember about the dangers associated with hoverboards being ridden irresponsibly, and how that might impact on Runnabout? We were told in the pre-seen that:

"These machines are not, however, without their risks, especially if they are operated irresponsibly. They can generally travel faster than a brisk walking pace, so the rider may have to navigate around pedestrians. The user could fall off or strike an obstacle if riding carelessly and a collision with a pedestrian would be potentially serious because the combined mass of the hoverboard and its user would have significant momentum when travelling at speed."

Also that:

"The software in Runnabout's hoverboards restricts the maximum speed of travel to 6 miles per hour (approximately 10 kilometres per hour). That is faster than a typical brisk walking pace of 3 to 4 miles per hour. The hoverboards could travel at much greater speeds, but Runnabout is concerned that a higher speed would lead to more accidents."

Furthermore:

"The insurance cost stated above refers to the insurance cover provided to users with respect to any injury caused by the user to a third party or damage to third party property. This cover applies automatically for the duration of any valid hire by a user. Runnabout also incurs significant cost for insurance against claims made against the company by users or by third parties for injury or property damage."

(2) Runnabout has identified on its schedule of Principal Risks that hoverboards can cause injury when ridden irresponsibly or at relatively high speed on pavements and in pedestrianised areas.

(3) Runnabout requires the permission of city authorities to operate; if that permission is withdrawn by any given city, then operations would have to cease.

Answering the question set – understanding the detail and linking to the requirements

The detail in the issue is given in the reference materials:

Reference Material

Geeland Daily News

Hoverboards hacked

Capital City Street Safety (CCSS), the local government department responsible for the safety of road users and pedestrians across Capital City, has issued a warning concerning a significant number of accidents involving Runnabout's rented hoverboards that had been modified by their users to operate at more than twice their intended maximum speed. During the past month, emergency services have been called to more than 40 incidents involving serious injury or significant property damage. Most of those incidents involved collisions between hoverboard users and pedestrians, but there have also been cases of hoverboard users injuring themselves through falling or riding into obstacles.

Most of these accidents have been blamed on users deactivating the safety settings on the hoverboard's onboard computer. Rented hoverboards have their speed restricted to 6 miles per hour, but a software hack can be purchased online and downloaded from the internet that cancels that setting and permits hoverboards to operate at their maximum speed of 15 miles per hour.

Hoverboards have USB ports that are used by Runnabout's qualified engineers to access sensor readings and run diagnostic routines. The software hack can be loaded onto a memory stick, which then overrides all speed restrictions when the memory stick is plugged into the USB port. The hoverboard then reverts to its restricted speed of 6 miles per hour when the memory stick is removed.

A CCSS spokesperson commented that hoverboards can be dangerous even at 6 miles per hour. Increasing the maximum speed to more than twice that was reckless. The spokesperson refused to comment on the possibility that CCSS might withdraw Runnabout's licence to operate shared-hoverboard services in Capital City.

Close

It is vital that you understand the nature and scope of the requirements. Here you need to draft a paper which covers the following:

- Firstly, identify and explain the interests of the key stakeholders

  Make sure you answer the question set – do not talk in just general terms about stakeholders and stakeholder management. You will no doubt recall Mendelow's matrix from your earlier studies, which is a model used to identify the level of power and interest of stakeholders in an organisation, and then how to manage each stakeholder grouping. This instruction is not asking for a general explanation of that model, or to use it in detail in answering this instruction. The examiner does not want to see a detailed explanation of the model, but it might be useful in generating ideas for your answer.

  Furthermore, the instruction lays out who are seen as the key stakeholders in respect of this issue – CCSS (and its counterparts in other cities), the emergency services, Runnabout's insurance company, and its users of hoverboards. You need to focus on these users in your answer – what are their respective interests in this matter?

  Furthermore, to "**explain**" is a higher level verb than "to identify". You need to make clear the precise nature of each stakeholder's interests – using the Mendelow measure of 'low' and 'high' can lend weight to your answer.

- Secondly, evaluate the proposal that the four executive directors should collectively own and manage the risk of users modifying our hoverboards.

  Evaluate in this context means to what extent you agree with the proposal, and to what extent do you disagree. After providing such analysis, you will then be in a position to form a conclusion.

Let's plan – Task 1(a)

If you prefer to plan within your answer box, then the above considerations will help you set up suitable headings and then start to populate them.

Alternatively, if you prefer to use your wipe clean whiteboard, then you could split your planning sheet into a grid to ensure all parts are covered:

Idea	Comments
Who are the key stakeholders?	
Comments specific to this particular issue	

Either way, you now need to brainstorm all the relevant points you can think of under the above headings, making sure you are bringing together your knowledge from the relevant syllabus as well as your analysis of the pre-seen information.

Let's think a bit more about this requirement by breaking them down into the component parts. For example:

Key stakeholder – the insurance company. Runnabout has a comprehensive policy that covers it for both injury and property damage. The premium charged by the insurance company will reflect on the risk of a pay-out under the policy, and the amount. The level of accidents has been rising recently due to the hacking of speed-limiting software, thereby increasing the risk. The insurance company therefore has high interest in this matter.

Specific comments – this results in the increased chances of having to pay out under the policy. At the time of the next renewal, a higher premium may need to be charged to compensate for increased risk, or possibly renewal of cover refused. It may also be possible to avoid pay-out on the grounds that cover is only for **valid** hire by a user – deliberately hacking the software renders the hire invalid.

Task 1(b)

Again you could set up headings within your answer or use a planning sheet:

Ideas	Comments
Reasons why you agree with the CEO's proposal	
Reasons why you don't agree with the CEO's proposal	

From your P3 knowledge, you will be aware that there is much that can be said on the subject of corporate governance – again, the key to answering this instruction well is not to just repeat generic theory, but to apply it to this situation. Governance is about ensuring that matters are well-managed – do you think that accepting responsibility collectively will result in fewer hacking incidents?

As a rough rule of thumb you should spend about 15–20% of the time available for reading and planning. So for this section of the exam, where you are given 60 minutes, you should be spending approximately 9–12 minutes planning your answer before you complete the exercise below. This would leave you about 45–50 minutes to write your answer and perhaps a few minutes spare to check through what you have written.

Exercise 1

Prepare a response to the first task for variant 1 of the May/August real exam, Runnabout.

4 Task 2

For task 2, the trigger and requirements are again mixed together into one screen, followed by reference material on a different screen:

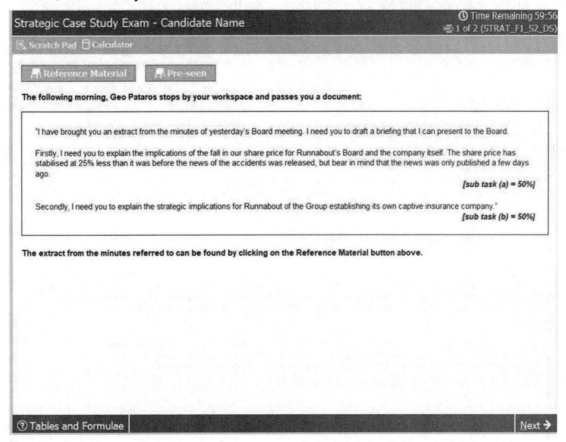

Understanding the context

With tasks like this, where there is little context given supporting the requirements, it is very important that you work carefully through the reference materials that accompany the instructions, so that you can tailor your ideas to the specific context in the question and not simply produce a generic answer.

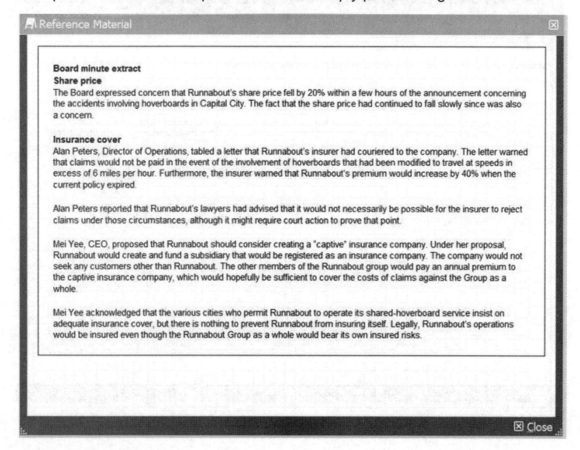

Reference Material

Board minute extract

Share price

The Board expressed concern that Runnabout's share price fell by 20% within a few hours of the announcement concerning the accidents involving hoverboards in Capital City. The fact that the share price had continued to fall slowly since was also a concern.

Insurance cover

Alan Peters, Director of Operations, tabled a letter that Runnabout's insurer had couriered to the company. The letter warned that claims would not be paid in the event of the involvement of hoverboards that had been modified to travel at speeds in excess of 6 miles per hour. Furthermore, the insurer warned that Runnabout's premium would increase by 40% when the current policy expired.

Alan Peters reported that Runnabout's lawyers had advised that it would not necessarily be possible for the insurer to reject claims under those circumstances, although it might require court action to prove that point.

Mei Yee, CEO, proposed that Runnabout should consider creating a "captive" insurance company. Under her proposal, Runnabout would create and fund a subsidiary that would be registered as an insurance company. The company would not seek any customers other than Runnabout. The other members of the Runnabout group would pay an annual premium to the captive insurance company, which would hopefully be sufficient to cover the costs of claims against the Group as a whole.

Mei Yee acknowledged that the various cities who permit Runnabout to operate its shared-hoverboard service insist on adequate insurance cover, but there is nothing to prevent Runnabout from insuring itself. Legally, Runnabout's operations would be insured even though the Runnabout Group as a whole would bear its own insured risks.

Close

Stop and think!

(1) Is there any technical knowledge that might help you to answer the instructions? Of the three strategic papers, this seems most relevant to F3 (share valuations) and E3 (strategy evaluation).

(2) What is your initial reaction to the proposal to set up an insurance company– does your 'gut feel' suggest that this is a good idea? Jot down initial thoughts.

Answering the question set – understanding the requirements

In this instance, you are not requested to put your answer into any particular format; the answer box has already been set up for you to write a response to Geo Pataros, so you only have to focus on answering the instructions set! As indicated already, CIMA don't give marks for formatting. There wouldn't be a penalty for failing to set the document up as a letter, email, report or whatever.

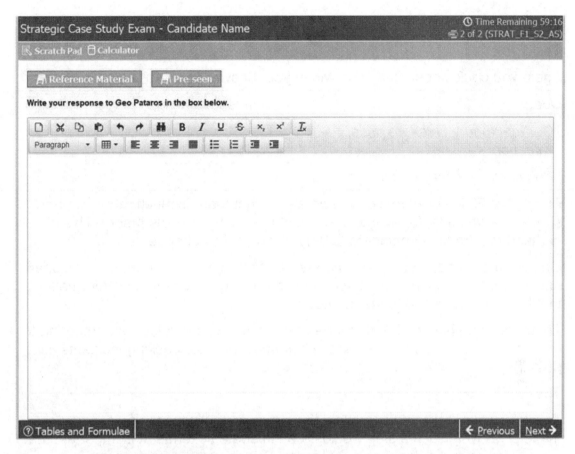

The precise instructions are:

- "Explain the implications of the fall in our share price for Runnabout's Board and the company itself. The share price has stabilised at 25% less than it was before the news of the accidents was released, but bear in mind that the news was only published a few days ago." As this is worth 50% of the marks for task 2, you should look to spend no more than 25 minutes on writing your answer to this instruction (remember, you will allow yourself 9-12 minutes to read and plan answers for task 2)

- "Explain the strategic implications of the Group establishing its own captive insurance company." This is also worth 50%, and so you should aim to complete the writing of this answer in around 25 minutes.

Let's plan!

Task 2(a)

Again you could set up headings within your answer or use a planning sheet:

Ideas	Comments
General theory on share price valuation	
Practical influences on share prices	

From your F3 knowledge, you will be aware that there is much theory on how shares are valued – for example, efficient market hypothesis theory. This can be used to introduce an understanding of why prices change.

On the other hand, you will also be aware of other, real-world impacts on share price moves e.g. short term speculators, time taken to digest new information that has been released to the market.

Try to focus on both of the above determinants of share value, remembering to make your comments as specific to Runnabout and the hacking incidents as possible.

Task 2(b)

This instruction asks you to explain the strategic implications i.e. to clarify or make clear what such a step would mean in strategic terms. It is important that you take note of the exact proposal – that Runnabout establish a new subsidiary, the sole purpose of which is to provide insurance cover to the Runnabout Group. This would be an act of diversification; at present, Runnabout's sole activity is hoverboard sharing services. What would such diversification mean for the company?

A suitable structure for your answer would appear to be:

- Identify reasons why you believe it would be a good response to the issue faced (taking into account your thoughts from task 1 when you addressed the interests of the current insurance company);

- Identify reasons why you believe it will not be a good response i.e. any problems it may encounter, or why this is not a suitable strategic response;

- End your answer with a conclusion – overall, do you think it will be viewed favourably as a response or not?

Exercise 2
Prepare a response to the second task.

5 Task 3

As for task 2, the trigger and requirements for task 3 are mixed together into one screen, together with reference material:

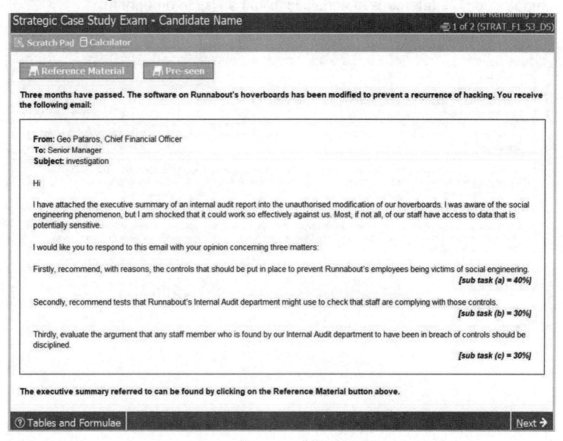

Understanding the context

After the appraisal that was conducted in tasks 1 and 2, it is clear that the case has taken a new turn, to examine the issue of controls and how the hack was perpetrated. The reference materials highlight an issue brought to management's attention by the internal audit function:

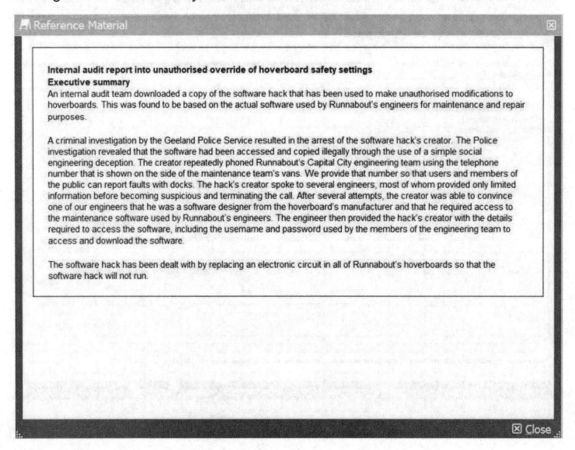

Internal audit report into unauthorised override of hoverboard safety settings

Executive summary

An internal audit team downloaded a copy of the software hack that has been used to make unauthorised modifications to hoverboards. This was found to be based on the actual software used by Runnabout's engineers for maintenance and repair purposes.

A criminal investigation by the Geeland Police Service resulted in the arrest of the software hack's creator. The Police investigation revealed that the software had been accessed and copied illegally through the use of a simple social engineering deception. The creator repeatedly phoned Runnabout's Capital City engineering team using the telephone number that is shown on the side of the maintenance team's vans. We provide that number so that users and members of the public can report faults with docks. The hack's creator spoke to several engineers, most of whom provided only limited information before becoming suspicious and terminating the call. After several attempts, the creator was able to convince one of our engineers that he was a software designer from the hoverboard's manufacturer and that he required access to the maintenance software used by Runnabout's engineers. The engineer then provided the hack's creator with the details required to access the software, including the username and password used by the members of the engineering team to access and download the software.

The software hack has been dealt with by replacing an electronic circuit in all of Runnabout's hoverboards so that the software hack will not run.

Stop and think!

- P3 would seem to provide the technical content for the 3 instructions – what can you remember about controls and tests of controls? What is meant by the term 'social engineering'?

- Although P3 has relevance to the third instruction, in some ways this would appear to be a general, commercial area, with little technical knowledge required to answer the question.

- Can you think of any practical responses to the safety of IT systems from your own place of work? What training are you made to undertake in order to recognise the risk and implications of social engineering? How would office morale be affected if disciplinary action followed an innocent mistake?

Answering the question set – understanding the requirements

There would appear to be no set format for this task; the template provided, together with the instruction screen, does not specify an email, letter, report etc. You can simply write your ideas in the box provided:

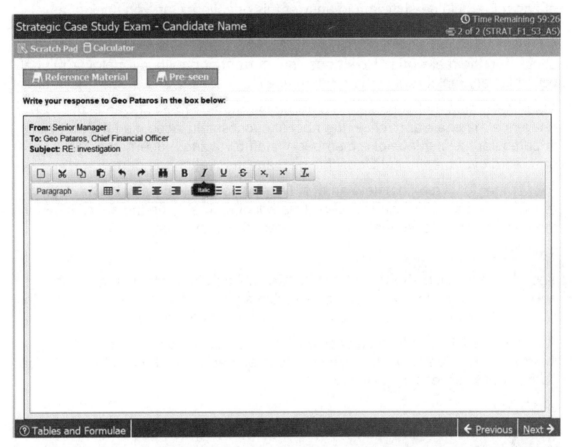

- Again, this task is allocated 60 minutes of time overall. You should spend 9-12 minutes reading and planning your answer to all 3 instructions, then allocate time to writing up your responses. This task has 3 separate instructions, so you will not be expected to spend as long on each one as in tasks 1 and 2. Instruction 1 is worth 40% of overall time, so writing your answer should take no longer than 20 minutes, with 15 minutes each for instructions 2 and 3.

- Instruction 1 can be broken down into 2 parts – recommend controls, with reasons. It is not enough to simply list a series of controls; you will also have to justify why each would be of benefit to Runnabout.

- Instruction 2 is asking for suggested tests of control that the Internal Audit function might use on the controls you suggest in instruction 1. It might therefore be of benefit to plan your response to these two instructions simultaneously.

- Instruction 3 is addressing a new topic (albeit related) and so can be planned as a separate instruction – again, an assessment of the advantages and disadvantages of such a proposal, before giving a conclusion, is the best approach.

Let's plan!

Task 3(a)

The first instruction is asking for controls to prevent employees from being the victims of social engineering. It is unlikely that a generic list of controls or types of controls would be sufficient to answer this question. Can you think of any instances where you have seen something similar before? Have you dealt with a question that has a similar theme? Or have you had experience of such controls in the real world? How does your current or previous employer(s) deal with this very real threat in the modern age?

Also, make sure that you use the detailed information that is given in the reference materials about how the hacker successfully accessed the software, in particular the instance of a member of staff divulging a username and password over the phone! Does this give any inspiration for ideas?

Remember to give a complete answer i.e. each control should also have the reason why it should be introduced. This will presumably be the specific benefit the control brings to Runnabout or the threat that it eliminates.

Task 3(b)

The mark allocation shows that this answer will be shorter than instruction 1 and, indeed, than any of the other instructions you have addressed so far in this case study – do not feel under pressure to write a huge amount of content!

As mentioned, this instruction should be considered in conjunction with instruction 1 – identify a control, justify its use, then think of a test that could be carried out to assess compliance.

Task 3(c)

As with the previous instruction, you do not have to write huge amounts here. Be practical in your advice – consider the long term impact on motivation of staff if such disciplinary action were to be introduced. How would it impact the relationship the Internal Audit function has with the rest of the organisation?

Exercise 3
Prepare a response to the third task.

6   Summary

You should now have a better understanding of how to approach the exam requirements and plan your answer. Although this chapter uses one particular exam as an example, the techniques used can be applied to any set of exam tasks.

Next steps:

(1)   As previously mentioned, you should attempt a written answer yourself to all of the tasks before reviewing the suggested solutions.

(2)   Reviewing the solutions may highlight knowledge gaps which you may need to revisit.

(3)   CIMA have released all exam variants, together with suggested responses and marking guides, for the May & August 2020 sittings, based on this pre-seen. You should try to attempt at least one more variant at exam speed and using the exam software if possible.

Test your understanding answers

These answers have been provided by CIMA for information purposes only. The answers created are indicative of a response that could be given by a good candidate. They are not to be considered exhaustive, and other appropriate relevant responses would receive credit.

CIMA will not accept challenges to these answers on the basis of academic judgement.

 ### Exercise 1

Requirement 1 – key stakeholders

CCSS and its counterparts have both high interest and high power. The high interest arises because they have a responsibility to manage and protect street safety. Preventable accidents reflect badly on them. The high power arises from the fact that the local governments in each city have the ability to restrict the use of hoverboards or even ban them completely. The Street Safety Departments will have little direct interest in the free and rapid flow of people on the pavements and so they will have little direct concern if hoverboards are banned in the interests of public safety. Runnabout should work to reassure these Departments that it will modify or adapt its hoverboards to prevent any recurrence of these modifications or, indeed, any other modifications that might be carried out. In the short term, it may be advisable for Runnabout to suspend services for a month until the ability to modify hoverboards has been eliminated.

The emergency services, particularly ambulance and police, have a high interest in these accidents because they consume resources when attending and investigating incidents. They have little direct power; the ambulance service is required to assist injured pedestrians regardless of the cause of their injuries and the police can only act if the law has been broken. Both services can, however, push national or local lawmakers for changes. Public sympathy would tend to support any such request. Runnabout should liaise with the emergency services, briefing them on the action that will be taken and asking whether there is anything further that might be done. It may be preferable to ensure that the emergency services are satisfied, even if that would make hoverboards less attractive to users.

The insurance company has both high interest and high power. The high interest comes from the fact that it must settle any insured losses and so there is potentially a significant financial loss if accident rates increase. The high power comes from the fact that the insurer might dispute liability because these accidents appear to have been the result of unauthorised modifications. Even if the question of liability is unclear, the insurer may deny liability in the first instance in order to force Runnabout to negotiate and possibly accept a reduced sum rather than risk the cost and uncertainty associated with taking court action.

The insurer will also be in a position to increase the premium paid by Runnabout. It would be impossible to trade in this business without insurance, so Runnabout would be forced to pay. It would be preferable for Runnabout to take a proactive approach to working with the insurance company to resolve matters, seeking to compromise over the wording and interpretation of the cover being provided.

Runnabout's users will probably be the most difficult stakeholder to deal with because there will be several groups, each with its own interest and power. Those users who modified the boards, either to speed up their daily commute or simply for the excitement of travelling at full speed, will be disappointed if the boards are modified to prevent this from happening. The other users will probably be indifferent because they do not wish to travel at excessive speed. The power of users varies according to the extent to which they are willing and able to use alternatives to hoverboards. Some users would effectively have little choice but to tolerate whatever modifications are made to Runnabout's hoverboards, while others may decide to switch to, say, shared-bicycle services instead. Arguably, Runnabout can do little to negotiate with users who might switch because the other stakeholders will undoubtedly demand that the hoverboards be modified so that restrictions on speed cannot be cancelled.

Requirement 2 – risk register

It could be argued that the Board has a collective responsibility for all risks that affect Runnabout and so the suggestion that four directors should share this risk may be realistic. The fact that the company was faced with an unexpected software challenge in this instance does not mean that future modifications will take the same form, so it may be desirable for staff from all backgrounds to be aware of the threat and to act accordingly. There may be a greater chance of uncovering problems before they become too serious if managers from all backgrounds are expected to share this responsibility and are actively looking for problems with hoverboards.

There is a danger that the assumption underlying this argument will prove to be unduly optimistic. Managers may not be alert to the threat of modification because they believe that colleagues from other functions will be better placed to look for it instead. There could be a risk of warning signs being overlooked or even ignored altogether and then managers wasting time in blaming colleagues for this failure.

The whole point of risk ownership is to ensure that there is a designated person or department that is responsible for dealing with a particular risk. Imposing a responsibility on a reluctant management team will still create a duty to monitor the threat, even if managers are concerned that they may be unable to do so effectively. Imposing this duty will force managers to take time out from other responsibilities to ensure that they are satisfied that unauthorised modifications are not a serious matter.

The response of the directors is disappointing and their attitude should not be encouraged. If the directors are unwilling to accept responsibility at an executive level then the managers who report to them may take the same view, which could lead to an inadequate response to the risk. If senior managers demonstrate a lack of commitment to the management of this risk then it is unlikely that their subordinates will.

Exercise 2

Requirement 1 – share price

The most immediate implication is that the shareholders may become discouraged because of the sudden and significant decline. A shareholder who had held Runnabout shares previously valued at, say G$10,000, will now own shares valued at only G$7,500, which could lead to the shareholders attempting to press the directors into finding an immediate response that restores the value of their shares. The shareholders may believe that the directors have been negligent in their management of the company and so they may start to think about a change in leadership. Even if the shareholders are not actually thinking in those terms, the directors may be concerned that their jobs are under threat and so they may be tempted to offer an urgent response that may not be fully thought through.

The fact that the fall in the share price has persisted for two days suggests that this is not a speculative "blip" arising from the concerns about the accident rate. It would appear that the stock market is concerned that future cash flows will be adversely affected by this news. If that is not the case, then Runnabout's Board could ensure that the shareholders are aware that the problems with the hoverboards can be remedied to the satisfaction of the city governments involved. If the capital markets can be reassured, then the share price will recover quickly.

The decrease in the share price will not have any direct impact on the company itself. The decrease is a loss to the shareholders. The decline in the share price reflects an increase in the cost of equity, so any future projects that will be financed by equity will have to deliver a higher return. The decline in valuation could, however, reflect the cost of any modifications or other actions that Runnabout will have to put into place in order to rectify its assets. If the markets were able to foresee a need to implement a programme of modifications to hoverboards or docks, then the cost of those modifications would have an immediate impact on the share price.

Runnabout could face the threat of a takeover if the shareholders are nervous about the future. The fall in share price means that anyone wishing to acquire a controlling interest will be able to do so for 25% less than would have been the case two days ago. It may also be possible to add further discouragement to the news and push the share price down even further. Runnabout could lose its independence and the Board could face replacement.

Requirement 2 – captive insurance company

A captive insurer could reduce operating costs significantly because the cost of insurance is high at present. The insurer's premium covers both the high level of the insured risk and also the need to make a profit on top of recovering expected costs. The creation of a captive insurer will enable Runnabout to obtain cover at its cost price, which should reduce the overall cost, provided there are no major unforeseen losses. The savings will enable Runnabout to maintain hire charges and so remain competitive with other forms of micromobility and public transport.

The captive insurer will give Runnabout much greater flexibility in terms of developing or modifying services. At present, the third-party insurance company might refuse to maintain cover if it is unsure about the consequences of any changes, whether planned or unplanned. The insurer's threat to increase its premium by 40% demonstrates the potentially disproportionate response to any changes in the risk profile of Runnabout's services. A captive insurer means that Runnabout will have a guarantee of the cover that it needs in order to be permitted to operate on public streets.

Runnabout may face regulatory problems in terms of obtaining the necessary licences and permissions required to operate an insurance company. There would be significant costs in terms of time and money in order to recruit suitably qualified management and staff. The various city authorities would undoubtedly have to accept the insurance arrangements as adequate before they would permit Runnabout to operate, which could require time and effort to support the authorities' due diligence before permitting Runnabout to proceed. The loss of key staff could also put Runnabout's status as an insurance company in some doubt.

Runnabout could face a catastrophic risk in the event of a significant number of unexpected claims against the internal insurer. At present, the third-party insurer must settle all insured losses arising throughout the life of the policy at no immediate cost to Runnabout. If Runnabout self-insures then it will be directly liable for any unexpected increase in accident rates or damage. Even so, that risk can be mitigated by Runnabout's ability to manage users' behaviour and, ultimately, to suspend services temporarily in order to deal with threats.

Exercise 3

Requirement 1 – social engineering

In this context, social engineering is essentially about having the ability to make contact with staff and influence them into revealing passwords and other information that could be used to obtain unauthorised access.

The most direct control would be to ensure that all staff are aware of the threat of social engineering and should be trained to deal with it. Ideally, all staff should receive training before they are granted any form of access to IT systems and that training should be refreshed, say, every two years. The training should warn staff that colleagues have no legitimate reason to request passwords, even if they are responsible for systems. Runnabout should make its staff personally responsible for any unauthorised access using their passwords in order to reinforce the need to maintain confidentiality.

Social engineering often relies on an intruder being able to create the impression that he or she works for the organisation. Anything that might validate a contact made from outside should be kept confidential as far as possible. For example, the internal telephone directory could be abused because it would enable an outsider to telephone a named individual and start a dialogue that could be convincing. Documents such as staff lists and telephone directories should be kept on secure web pages that require valid user names and passwords to access.

Staff should be discouraged from revealing that they work for Runnabout in their social media profiles and posts because that could provide outsiders with insights that could make it easier to trick them into believing that they are colleagues. It should also be forbidden to use Runnabout staff email addresses for personal business because that could provide yet further access to outsiders. Staff should be required to report any suspicious contacts that suggest that an attempt is being made to penetrate the company's systems so that vigilance can be increased. Staff should be trained not to respond to suspicious emails or to click on any links that they contain in case that confirms to the outsider that they have a valid email address.

Requirement 2 – internal audit

The Internal Audit Department should be able to examine files and documents to ensure that training is being provided and that staff acknowledge their responsibilities. For example, Runnabout should ask staff to sign an acknowledgement that they are aware of the need to safeguard their passwords and internal audit should review documents for a random sample of staff to ensure that they have signed. There should also be evidence that staff have completed training on schedule. The simplest way to do that would be to offer online training that is supported by objective test questions after each section has been read. Runnabout's internal auditors should be able to select a sample of staff and check that they have completed the training and achieved a satisfactory pass.

Runnabout's internal auditors might conduct online searches of social media sites using accounts created for test purposes. Inputting "Runnabout" into a site's search engine might pick up a large number of posts by users, but it would not take long for the members of the audit team to read through those in order to check whether they appear to be posts by Runnabout staff. The audit team might search on "@runnabout.com" in order to identify any cases of staff using their work email addresses for personal business.

The most complex audit test would be to conduct a penetration test on Runnabout's systems. That would involve members of Internal Audit contacting staff by phone or by email to ask for usernames, passwords or other useful information. If the Internal Audit Department succeeded in gaining access then the controls are not acting properly and further work will be required. Regardless of the outcome, Runnabout's staff should be informed of the results, partly as a deterrent against releasing information in the future, for fear of being caught by Internal Audit conducting a repeat penetration test.

Requirement 3 – disciplinary action

It is important that all staff are aware that Runnabout's Board regards any control breaches as a serious matter. It may be sufficient for the supervisors of the departments that have been audited to be made aware of any failures and for them to be made responsible for counselling the staff who were responsible for breaches. The most important issue is to communicate the fact that compliance is scrutinised and taken seriously and that any breaches will be followed up.

There is a risk that a disproportionate response to any breach will lead to staff becoming demotivated and possibly even leaving. Experienced staff may be at greater risk of overlooking rules and procedures because they may become overfamiliar and overconfident. Those are precisely the staff whom Runnabout's Board should aim to retain and encourage to use their strengths to the best of their abilities.

Runnabout's Board should also aim to prevent Internal Audit from becoming associated with disciplinary action, otherwise staff may not cooperate during Internal Audit investigations. The focus of any response to compliance failures should be to point out any shortcomings and recommend an appropriate remedy for the future. Disciplinary action would only be necessary in the case of repeated or malicious misbehaviour or a refusal to comply with requirements in the future

Feedback on the real exam and tips on answering tasks on the more technical aspects of F3

Chapter learning objectives

To understand how to improve the quality of answers when sitting a Strategic Case Study exam, and to understand how to answer the more technical aspects of F3.

1 Summary of exams to date

1.1 Examiner's feedback

After each exam sitting CIMA publish the exams, suggested answers, summary marking guides and an examiner's report that discusses all variants from that sitting.

While many students are producing high quality scripts in the time available, there are common themes that have arisen where students can improve. Here are the Examiner's reports from 2 exams set in 2019, the February and May sittings, and also for the May/August 2020 sittings:

May 2019 – Examiner's report

Candidate performance

Overall, candidates performed reasonably well on some aspects of all the variants. However, there were a number of areas of concern relating to student performance in several other areas; this applies to all variants. The main weaknesses were that in several tasks, candidates failed to apply their knowledge directly to the scenario information and in some parts candidates just failed to answer what had been asked. On the positive side most candidates structured their answers well.

All answers must be applied to the case study and should bring in aspects of the pre-seen information as well as the information and exhibits in the unseen material. Most candidates did demonstrate application of knowledge which was good. Many candidates' answers lacked depth of development and therefore, although demonstrating a basic understanding and application of knowledge, they failed to accumulate sufficient marks due to not developing their answers sufficiently.

Candidates are reminded to carefully read each task requirement and only answer what has been asked. In addition, candidates are also reminded that theoretical answers are awarded very few marks.

Looking ahead to future examinations

Candidates should read the pre-seen material carefully and come into the examination understanding the industry and the company which will be the focus of the exam. This will help candidates formulate good answers that relate to the tasks they are given.

Candidates must manage their time well and make sure they do not run out of time on sections they know well.

Candidates must read the questions very carefully and answer what has been asked. Answers which are not applied to the case will not score high marks.

A good level of knowledge of the three strategic syllabi is necessary in order to do well in the exams. It is not enough to have knowledge of topics; candidates must be able to apply their knowledge to a variety of situations and show they have an in-depth knowledge of the subject matter.

February 2019 – Examiner's report

Candidate performance

Overall, candidates performed reasonably well on some aspects of all the variants. However, there were a number of areas of concern relating to student performance in several other areas; this applies to all variants. The main weaknesses were that in several tasks, candidates failed to apply their knowledge directly to the scenario information and in some parts candidates just failed to answer what had been asked. In many cases candidates quoted and described models but did not apply them to the case study; this approach does not gain marks.

All answers must be applied to the case study and should bring in aspects of the pre-seen information as well as the information and exhibits in the unseen material. Answers which are purely rote learning were quite common in some requirements and this approach is awarded very few marks. Many candidates' answers lacked depth of development and therefore, although demonstrating a basic understanding and application of knowledge, failed to accumulate sufficient marks due to insufficient development of answers.

Candidates are reminded to carefully read each task requirement and only answer what has been asked. In addition, candidates are also reminded that theoretical answers are awarded very few marks.

Looking ahead to future examinations

Candidates should read the pre-seen material carefully and come into the examination understanding the industry and the company which will be the focus of the exam. This will help candidates formulate good answers that relate to the tasks they are given.

Candidates must manage their time well and make sure they do not run out of time on sections they know well.

Candidates must read the questions very carefully and answer what has been asked. Answers which are not applied to the case will not score high marks.

A good level of knowledge of the three strategic syllabi is necessary in order to do well in the exams. It is not enough to have knowledge of topics; candidates must be able to apply their knowledge to a variety of situations and show they have an in-depth knowledge of the subject matter.

May/August 2020 – Examiner's report

As always, the key to achieving a passing mark or better is to answer the question as set. Higher marks are awarded to fuller answers that are relevant and correct.

To achieve a level 3 in most traits it was expected that a candidate would demonstrate good technical understanding of the topic being tested through clear and comprehensive discussion and where asked justify their answer; the answer should of course be applied to Runnabout and the particular scenario within the task. That is particularly important at the Strategic level because corporate strategy must be matched to the entity and the business that it operates in. If a candidate scored at a level 1 on a trait it is likely that they did one or all of the following:

- Failed to address the requirement when answering the question.

- Demonstrated limited technical understanding, possibly with gaps in knowledge or understanding.

- Provided insufficient justification for arguments.

- Failed to reflect the scenario or the specifics of Runnabout in their answer.

The comments for the November 2020/February 2021 sittings were identical to those of May/August 2020.

1.2 Lessons to be learnt from the above feedback

Whilst it might be argued that feedback has been mentioned from just 6 exam sittings and therefore represents a limited sample, the comments made above are recurrent themes in almost all examiner feedback reports. Students should look to take notice of all the relevant points made in the reports illustrated if they are to maximise their chances of success in this exam.

So, what are the learning points that we might take from the above reports?

- **Application of knowledge is critical**

  The examiners at Strategic Case Study are not testing how good your knowledge of the strategic syllabi is; you have already proved this by passing the three papers of E3, F3 and P3. Case study is a different exercise; what is now being demanded is whether you can *apply* this knowledge in a particular situation. Simply demonstrating rote learning, and therefore producing answers that look as though they may have come straight out of a study text, is not going to achieve sufficient marks for a pass.

- **Consider the pre-seen as well as the unseen material**

  The pre-seen material is deliberately released to students well in advance of the actual exam. This is to allow them to absorb the information that is contained within, to build up a bigger picture of the business that features within the case and the industry it operates in, and to perform some research on the industry itself. It should not then be ignored as soon as the examination begins! As well as containing the instructions, the unseen examination paper contains fresh materials that help to put the pre-seen into a more up to date context; students should therefore bear in mind how what they learnt from the pre-seen has now become better defined when they read the fresh materials.

- **Answers need depth of development**

  This means that often students do not develop their ideas sufficiently to gain good marks. They begin an answer by demonstrating good knowledge and even application of that knowledge, but do not then develop the ideas sufficiently.

  For example, say that a new competitor has just emerged, and is having an impact on the business that you work for. A candidate might suggest that, from a Porter's Five Forces analysis, the threat of new entrants would appear to be low, hence the new issue that there is a new competitive threat – at this point, the candidate is demonstrating knowledge. The candidate should then go on to talk about what this means for the business going forwards – will there be downwards pressure on profit margins? Are there likely to be added pressures from additional new entrants to the market? What unique selling points (USPs) can the business use to counteract the new threat? Is this likely to be an ongoing problem? What other advice would you give to the leadership team?

  It is only through proper development of ideas that students can hope to achieve good marks for insightful analysis.

- **Each task requirement must be read carefully**

  Sometimes it is possible to look at an instruction in an exam, think you have understood what is being asked of you, and then write a full and comprehensive answer (or so you believe!) only to realise subsequently that you have not scored as well as you might have hoped. This is most probably because you have failed to answer the question that was set. It may well be that you have produced an excellent response to a slightly different question, but the examiner cannot give you credit for this – you will only be judged on your ability to answer the precise instructions set to all candidates.

  It is therefore well worth investing time in reading through each task requirement very carefully, looking at the precise instructions that have been put forward. Think of the verbs that have been used, and refer back to the hierarchy of verbs that CIMA has used throughout your examination studies. Also, how many instructions are there? It may appear at first glance that you are being asked to do just one thing, but closer examination shows that there are actually two instructions in one.

  For example, if a task asks you to "Identify and evaluate", this will require you to pick up on matters that are relevant (identify) and then assess what the implications are for the business, possibly even concluding on the significance of the issue (evaluate).

- **Go into the exam understanding the industry**

  It is very important that you carry out some background research on the industry that features in your pre-seen. This will help you develop a much better appreciation of the broader issues facing the business that you work for, and may even point towards some of the themes that will feature in each of the five variants of the exam. Remember, the examiner has to derive inspiration from somewhere for writing exam questions – where better than the real world!

  For example, in the May 2019 exam Denby Healthcare (which was considered in chapter 2 of this text), an issue that was highlighted in the pre-seen was that of the local National Health Service using private hospital resources to ensure that patients did not have to wait any longer for treatment than the guidelines that the government had publicised. This then formed the outline of variant 2 of the exam.

  A student who had conducted industry research would have come across a wealth of information on this very topic. For example, consider the following:

  www.nhs.uk/common-health-questions/nhs-services-and-treatments/do-i-need-a-gp-referral-for-private-treatment/#

  https://www.bma.org.uk/-/media/files/pdfs/practical%20advice%20at%20work/ethics/interfaceguidanceethicsmay2009.pdf

  www.nhs.uk/common-health-questions/nhs-services-and-treatments/if-i-pay-for-private-treatment-how-will-my-nhs-care-be-affected/

  Great sources for information include the BBC, YouTube, online newspapers (the Guardian allows free access), and real world companies (for the Denby Healthcare case, it would have served students well to look at organisations such as BUPA, Nuffield Healthcare, and the Spire, as well as other organisations). Naturally, Google is also very useful.

  Having said this, do not worry if you do not pick up on a particular article or web page as part of your research! Candidates who did not pick up on a particular item should still be able to write a good answer based on their technical knowledge, their study of the pre-seen and reading of the unseen

- **Manage time well**

  It is interesting to note that time management overall does not appear to be a problem in Case Study; 3 hours would seem perfectly sufficient to answer the instructions that are set. However, the examiner sees evidence of students coming across a task that they are clearly confident with, and then spending far too long on creating an answer that is excessive.

Success in case study is about making a decent attempt at **all** of the instructions set; you will find it very difficult to pass through providing a detailed answer to one instruction, and only a very brief or shallow answer to another. Use the time guidance given on the opening screen of the exam to determine how long you should spend on each instruction, and stick to it.

For example, in the previous chapter, the May/August 2020 exam variant 1 on Runnabout contained the following information on the first screen:

Section (task)	Time for section (minutes)	Number of answer screens	Number of sub-tasks	% time to spend on each sub-task
1	60	1	2	(a) 60% (b) 40%
2	60	1	2	(a) 50% (b) 50%
3	60	1	3	(a) 40% (b) 30% (c) 30%

This would therefore mean that, for task 1 which has a total of 60 minutes allocated to it, candidates should spend 60% of that time on sub-task a), and 40% on sub-task b). This means no more than 36 minutes on the first sub-task and the rest on the second. The examiner will be thinking about the amount of content expected for each sub-task and will therefore provide such guidance accordingly. Ignoring such advice is high risk!

2 Answering more technical aspects of F3

2.1 Introduction

In the November 2018 report, the examiner made the following comment:

"There are always F pillar questions, and they always by far the weakest answers."

This is not the only occasion that such a comment has been made in the Examiner's report. It should therefore be asked what students can do to improve in such requirements. In the next section we consider an example of such a task from the May 2019 exam.

You may wish to revisit chapter 2 at this point to refresh your memory on what the Denby Healthcare case involved.

2.2 Variant 1, task 1

The second instruction to this task would have addressed core activity 3 of the syllabus, Recommend financing strategies, with the associated assessment outcome of "I can recommend suitable sources of finance"

Scenario

- Denby would look to establish specialist 'Denby Sports Injury Centres' at its hospitals

- It would need to raise $130 million of fresh finance to fund this.

The requirement

"Would it be irresponsible for Denby's Board to borrow the K$130 million required for this purpose?"

Possible answer approach/structure

As mentioned earlier, it is vital that students correctly interpret the instruction that is given. It would be easy to misinterpret this task if looked at only briefly; for example, it could be interpreted as "How might Denby's Board raise the K$130 million required for this purpose?"

That is not what the question is asking!

If a student had interpreted the requirement in this way, then a logical structure would have been:

1   Talk about equity finance

- Start with a general explanation of how equity might be raised – retained earnings, squeezing working capital, rights issue, new equity issue.

- Then perhaps comment on the pros and cons of equity finance – how it might affect control for shareholders, the greater flexibility it can present to cash flows (no obligation to pay a dividend), the different levels of cost associated with each source, etc.

2   Talk about debt finance

- Then move on to talk about debt, and how this might be raised – a term loan, leasing or perhaps debentures.

- Next, comment on the pros and cons of debt finance – the tax shield on interest, the lower cost to the company compared to equity, the obligation to pay interest each year, etc.

3   Conclusion

- Finally, conclude on which source is preferable for Denby Healthcare.

Unfortunately, the above approach would have been guilty of many of the criticisms mentioned when reviewing the examiner's reports at the start of this chapter. It began badly when the student failed to answer the question actually set, and soon turned into a general discussion of sources of finance as opposed to one that is tailored to Denby Healthcare itself.

Suggested answer approach/structure

Again, correct interpretation of the task is vital. What is the question asking students to do?

It is asking if raising the finance required via debt is 'irresponsible'. This means is it an appropriate way to raise the finance, and what impact might it have on the company? It is not asking for a detailed examination of equity.

A suggested structure might therefore be:

1 Talk about the impact on financial gearing

- Look at the current gearing level of Denby Healthcare, and consider how a further K$130 million of debt would affect this. Would it make the financial gearing levels excessive? How might key stakeholders, such as shareholders, react?

- You could also look at the statement of profit and loss; how might the extra debt impact on a key ratio such as interest cover? Would the company's overall profitability be put at risk with extra interest payable obligations?

2 Talk about what Denby would have to pay to secure the debt

- What is likely to be a lender's required rate of return? Does Denby have assets to offer as security to reduce the risk to the lender, thereby reducing the rate of interest payable on the debt?

3 Conclusion

- After considering the above, is taking on the finance in the form of debt 'irresponsible'? Might equity be a better proposal? If so, justify **briefly** such a comment.

Examiner's comments

The question essentially raised two related issues. Borrowing to fund this project will increase gearing. That raises questions about whether the gearing ratio is likely to be raised beyond acceptable limits. Better candidates should have recognised that gearing will increase, but not to the extent that there is a categorical argument that it has become excessive.

The increase in gearing should have been considered against the possibility that the new venture will have an adverse effect on operating profit. It should always be recognised that high gearing is a problem because it intensifies the effect of volatility in operating profit on the profit for the year. If there is no volatility in operating profit then gearing is much less of an issue.

Candidates might also have considered whether lenders would be prepared to accept Denby's assets as security. They may have limited resale value, if a lender could accept the bad publicity associated with foreclosing on a hospital and removing potentially life-saving equipment. This question was done quite well by many candidates with many discussing gearing well. Weaker candidates did not mention gearing at all. Few candidates mentioned the issue of using assets as security which was disappointing. Some candidates decided to say that equity would be better and gave a whole answer on equity, which did not gain high marks.

2.3 Variant 2, task 3

The third instruction to this task would have addressed core activity 3 of the syllabus, Recommend financing strategies, with the associated assessment outcome of "I can recommend dividend policy."

Scenario

- Denby would look to buy 4 hospitals in need of refurbishment to bring them up to acceptable standard. The cost of these hospitals would be a nominal K$1

- Denby would then invest K$250 million in refurbishment.

- This would result in the new hospitals being referred National Health Service patients exclusively, and the whole Denby Group being treated as a preferred supplier.

- If Denby did not proceed with this proposal, it could use some of its considerable cash reserves to pay a significant dividend to shareholders.

The requirement

"How would the payment of a significant dividend affect shareholder wealth?"

Suggested answer approach/structure

Once again, it is important to recognise that this question is not asking you to recite everything you know about dividend policy; the trap you could easily fall into is to write about Modigliani and Miller's ideas compared to the traditional viewpoint, and then conclude with some practical suggestions.

Focus on the instruction: "How would the payment of a significant dividend affect shareholder wealth?"

To paraphrase the instruction, in what ways might paying a significant dividend increase shareholder wealth, and in what ways might it reduce it?

A suggested structure is therefore:

1   <u>Talk about shareholder wealth</u>

- Returns to shareholders from equity investments come in two forms – a dividend income stream, and capital gain in the value of their investment.

- A significant dividend may certainly have a positive effect on shareholder wealth in the short term – more return is being received than anticipated.

2   <u>Talk about impact on share price</u>

- How will the market react to the payment of a large dividend? It might perceive that the increased level will be typical of the future, and so a short term increase results; if the new level cannot be maintained in future, it will probably fall again. This results in share price volatility, which shareholders typically do not like.

- Shareholders might feel that a company such as Denby needs to keep investing to fund future growth, and that paying a significant dividend might reduce such possibilities. In this case, the share price is likely to fall.

3   Other matters

- Investors will have different preferences on how wealth is increased, depending on their tax position; some investors may prefer income, others capital gain.

- Much will depend on how news of the dividend is released to the market. If it is clearly explained that this is a one-off extra payment, the share price is likely to remain stable.

Examiner's comments

This requirement was answered reasonably well by candidates, many of whom were able to present a sound discussion of the implications of paying a large dividend to its shareholders. Good answers also included points relating to the tax considerations of shareholders.

Weaker answers were those that merely considered that the markets may be misled as to the level of future dividends.

2.4 Variant 5, task 2

The second instruction to this task would have addressed core activity 3 of the syllabus, Recommend financing strategies, with the associated assessment outcome of "I can recommend dividend policy."

Scenario

- Denby would look to buy BNC, a nursing college in the country of Bordia. Acquiring BNC could ensure that Denby has a reliable source of competent nurses.

- BNC is still owned by its founders, and is unquoted. Denby has many current nurses that were trained at BNC on its three year programme.

- BNC receives no state funding; its income is earned solely from fees paid by nurses for courses.

- BNC barely breaks even due to the high cost of running nursing degrees.

The requirement

"What basis should we use to determine the value of BNC to Denby?"

Suggested answer approach/structure

This question is not asking you to recite everything you know about valuation techniques. It is asking you to apply your knowledge of such matters to this specific circumstance. You should therefore ask yourself what techniques might be relevant here.

You might start by asking yourself what techniques exist. You will probably consider the following:

- Net assets approach

- Dividend based

- Use of a price/earnings (P/E) ratio

- Discounted future cash flows

A suggested structure is therefore:

1   Introduce valuation techniques, and dismiss those likely to be irrelevant

- As BNC is barely breaking even, it is unlikely to be paying dividends, and so the dividend valuation model is not relevant. Also, this is more useful for valuing a minority stake.

- Similarly, if there is little profit, using a P/E multiple will result in a very low number.

- This therefore leaves the net assets approach and discounted future cash flows as potentially relevant.

2   Talk about the net assets approach

- What are the likely assets of BNC? Possibly premises and training equipment, which gives a tangible value, but the largest asset of a training organisation is surely the staff (and possibly the business' reputation) – neither of these will be on the balance sheet, and so adjustment would need to be made.

- Net assets could also indicate the maximum Denby should be prepared to pay, as this represents the opportunity cost of acquisition (Denby could, alternatively, set up a business like BNC from scratch).

3   Talk about discounted cash flows

- Whilst profits might be low, BNC may still generate positive cash flows (low profits could be due to issues such as impairments). This would suggest BNC has some value.

- Future cash flows should incorporate synergies that result from the acquisition e.g. Denby saving on recruitment fees.

4   Conclusion

- Using both measures will give Denby a range of values upon which to base a negotiation with the current owners of BNC.

Examiner's comments

Many answers were a little weak as they failed to use the information given in the scenario. Many candidates identified the weakness of the financial performance of BNC and valued the business very simply as future cash flows. However, there were some excellent response to this requirement.